The Handbook

of

Indulgences

THE HANDBOOK
OF
INDULGENCES
—
NORMS AND GRANTS
—

AUTHORIZED ENGLISH EDITION

CATHOLIC BOOK PUBLISHING CORP.

NEW YORK

Concordat cum originali:
Ronald F. Krisman

Published by authority of the Bishops' Committee on the Liturgy,
National Conference of Catholic Bishops.

ACKNOWLEDGMENTS

This edition is based on the Third edition of the *Enchiridion Indulgentiarum: Normae et Concessiones* of May 1986 (First edition — June 1968, Second edition — October 1968) published by Libreria Editrice Vaticana. © 1986 Libreria Editrice Vaticana, Città del Vaticana. All rights reserved.

The English translation of excerpts of prayer no. 37 from *The Roman Missal* © 1973, International Committee on English in the Liturgy, Inc. (ICEL); the English translation of prayers nos. 1 to 10, 21, 22, 24, 26, 27, 29, 31, 32, 39, 40, 44, 46, 47, 51 to 53, 57, 59, 62, 64, and parts of the Appendix: Pious Invocations from *A Book of Prayer* © 1982, ICEL; the English translation of the Decree of the Apostolic Penitentiary, of the Apostolic Constitution *Indulgentiarum doctrina*, and excerpts from the English translation of Norms on Indulgences from *Documents on the Liturgy, 1963 — 1979: Conciliar, Papal, and Curial Texts* © 1982, ICEL; excerpt from *Presidential Prayers for Experimental Use at Mass* © 1983, ICEL; the English translation of prayer no. 70, Renewal of Baptismal Promises, from the *Rite of Christian Initiation of Adults* © 1986, ICEL. All rights reserved.

Scripture selections are taken from *The New American Bible with Revised New Testament and Psalms* © 1991, 1986, and 1970, the Confraternity of Christian Doctrine, Washington, DC, and are used by license of the copyright owner. All rights reserved.

The brief excerpts from Vatican II found on pages 27-34 are taken (with slight modifications for inclusive language) from *Vatican Council II, Conciliar and Post Conciliar Documents*, edited by Austin Flannery, O.P. © 1975, 1984, 1986, 1987 and are used by permission of Costello Publishing Company, Northport, N.Y. All rights reserved.

The text of the hymn "Come, Creator Spirit" on pp. 86-87 (taken from *Hymnbook 1982* © 1982, The Church Hymnal Corporation) is © by John Webster Grant. All rights reserved.

DECREE OF THE APOSTOLIC PENITENTIARY

Prot. 77/88/I

This Apostolic Penitentiary raises no objection to the publication of the present English version of the *Handbook of Indulgences*. Furthermore, although it is the result of the praiseworthy efforts of the National Conference of Catholic Bishops of the United States of America, the Apostolic Penitentiary asks the Conference to permit this English version to be published in joint cooperation with the episcopal conferences of other nations in which the English language is used. In doing so, copyright laws should be respected.

Given at Rome at the Apostolic Penitentiary, 8 November 1988.

✠ Aloysius Cardinal Dadaglio,
Major Penitentiary

Aloysius De Magistris, *Regent*

CONTENTS

CONTENTS

PREFACE TO THE THIRD EDITION

On 29 June 1968, the solemnity of the apostles Peter and Paul, the Apostolic Penitentiary published the first edition of *The Handbook of Indulgences*. Since that date great strides and important changes have taken place in matters of Church discipline, in the celebration of the sacred rites, and especially in the use of the Word of God. From the latter in particular the entire life of the Church has marvelously benefited.

During this same period the following events have had some impact worth noting as regards indulgences: the publication of the Neo-Vulgate edition of the Scriptures; the publication of new ritual books and texts for liturgical celebrations; and, finally, the promulgation of the new Code of Canon Law for the Latin Church.

To be sure, the new Code has but expressly confirmed the prescriptions already contained in the special laws already issued concerning the use and the granting of indulgences. So even though all these mentioned events have not basically changed anything concerning the discipline on indulgences, nevertheless these new publications and norms should be taken into account in order rightly to express those norms and in order to furnish a listing of the works and prayers endowed with an indulgence. Such have to be considered when there is need to cite the sacred scriptures, to indicate the current regulations for liturgical actions, or to refer to the new canons and their numbering.

It was therefore decided that there was a need to prepare a new edition based upon the criteria mentioned above. In this way *The Handbook of Indulgences* would then be in harmony with other authentic texts which have liturgical and canonical force. And, since the occasion furnished itself, it was also decided that it would be a good time to add some new indulgenced grants which had been issued by Pope John Paul II. He approved this present edition during an audience on 13 December 1985.

11

For purposes of historical accuracy this third edition also includes the apostolic constitution *Indulgentiarum doctrina* so that it can be seen that what is found in the original document has undergone no change. For similar reasons this edition also contains before its Introduction the text of the Decree of the Apostolic Penitentiary dated 29 June 1968 so that the criteria which determine the canonical force of *The Handbook* are clearly evident.

In publishing this third edition of *The Handbook of Indulgences,* the Apostolic Penitentiary earnestly hopes that the faithful are greatly aided in their quest for holiness, whether through their devout use of indulgences or through their zeal for the charity and good works which are the very root and foundation for indulgences.

Given at Rome at the Apostolic Penitentiary, 18 May 1986, the solemnity of Pentecost.

✠ Aloysius Cardinal Dadaglio,
Major Penitentiary

Aloysius De Magistris, *Regent*

DECREE OF THE APOSTOLIC PENITENTIARY

In the Apostolic Constitution *Indulgentiarum doctrina* of 1 January 1967 we read: "The Church at this time has seen fit to introduce new elements and decree new norms with regard to indulgences in order to enhance the value of this practice and the esteem for it."

Norm 13 of the Constitution establishes this: "The *Enchiridion indulgentiarum* is to be revised with a view to attaching indulgences only to major prayers and devotional, penitential, and charitable works."

In obedience to the will of Pope Paul VI as expressed both through the Apostolic Constitution *Indulgentiarum doctrina* and through later enactments, this Apostolic Penitentiary has carefully seen to the compilation of a new *Enchiridion indulgentiarum*.

After receiving the report of the undersigned Cardinal Major Penitentiary at an audience on 14 June 1968, Pope Paul VI has on 15 June 1968 approved the new *Enchiridion indulgentiarum* printed by the Vatican Press. He has ordered it to be the authoritative collection; suppressed are all general grants of indulgences not incorporated into the new *Enchiridion* as well as all the legislation on indulgences of the *Codex Iuris Canonici*, of apostolic letters, even motu proprios, and of decrees of the Holy See that are not included among the Norms for indulgences in this *Enchiridion*.

All things to the contrary notwithstanding, even those meriting explicit mention.

Given at Rome at the Apostolic Penitentiary, 29 June 1968, the solemnity of the holy Apostles Peter and Paul.

✠ Joseph Cardinal Ferretto,
*Titular Bishop of the Suburban Church of Sabina
and Poggio Mirteto,
Major Penitentiary*

John Sessolo, *Regent*

INTRODUCTION

1. The publication of this Handbook fulfills the directive found in norm 13 of the apostolic constitution, *Indulgentiarum doctrina:* "The *Enchiridion indulgentiarum* is to be revised with a view to attaching indulgences only to major prayers and devotional, penitential, and charitable works."

2. With appreciation for both tradition and the changes of recent times, what principle should be used in judging certain prayers and works to be outstanding ones? Particularly appropriate would be those prayers and works which not only help the faithful satisfy for punishment due their sins but also and especially urge them on to a more fervent charity. This is the principle upon which this revision is based.[1]

3. Participation in the sacrifice of the Mass and in the sacraments is not enriched with any indulgences. The reason is that tradition teaches that they far outstrip any other activity as regards their efficacy in "sanctifying and purifying."[2]

But the reception of first holy communion, the celebration of a first Mass by a newly ordained priest, the celebration of the Mass which closes a eucharistic congress, etc., are special occasions. Such occasions warrant the granting of an indulgence. But the latter is not so much attached to the participation in the Mass or the sacraments as it is to the extraordinary circumstances surrounding such participation. In this way an indulgence is employed to promote and, as it were, to reward the devotional zeal which characterizes such celebrations, which provides good example to others, and which honors the sublime eucharist and the priesthood.

Tradition also teaches, however, that an indulgence can be attached to various works of private and public devotion. Therefore such works of charity and repentance which ought to be given greater emphasis in our times can be en-

---

[1] Cf. the Allocution of Pope Paul VI to the College of Cardinals and to the Roman Curia, 23 December 1966 (AAS, 59 [1967]: 57).

[2] Cf. Paul VI, Apostolic Constitution *Indulgentiarum doctrina,* 1 January 1967, no. 11.

riched with an indulgence. But all such works endowed with indulgences should never in any way be set aside or apart from the Mass and the sacraments. The Mass and the sacraments remain *the* outstanding sources of sanctification and purification[3]—no matter how good any such indulgenced works and patiently endured sufferings may be. Such good works and sufferings become the faithful's offering which is joined to Christ's offering in the eucharistic sacrifice.[4] In this matter it is the Mass and the sacraments themselves which lead the faithful to carry out the responsibilities placed on them so that "they put into action in their lives what they have received in faith."[5] And, conversely, it is by carefully carrying out their responsibilities that they become better disposed day by day to participate fruitfully in the Mass and the sacraments.[6]

4. In light of the changed conditions of our times this *Handbook* puts more emphasis on the action of the Christian faithful (the *opus operantis)* than on the devotional works themselves (the *opus operatum).* For that reason you will not find here any long list of such works, as if they could be separated from the everyday life of the Christian faithful. You will find given, however, a short list of indulgenced works.[7] That list contains those works considered more effective in urging the Christian faithful to lead more useful and holier lives so that no longer will there exist "that pernicious opposition between professional and social activity on the one hand, and religious life on the other . . . but there will exist an integration of human, domestic, professional, scientific, and technical enterprises with religious values, under whose supreme direction all things are ordered to the glory of God."[8]

---

[3] Cf. Paul VI, Apostolic Constitution *Indulgentiarum doctrina,* no. 11.

[4] Cf. Second Vatican Council, Dogmatic Constitution on the Church *Lumen gentium,* no. 34.

[5] Roman Missal, Oration, Monday within the octave of Easter.

[6] Cf. Second Vatican Council, Constitution on the Liturgy *Sacrosanctum Concilium,* art. 9-13.

[7] Cf. below, especially nos. I-III, pp. 16-23.

[8] Cf. Second Vatican Council, Pastoral Constitution on the Church in the Modern World *Gaudium et spes,* no. 43 (Flannery translation).

Great care has been taken to put more emphasis on Christian living and on the formation of a spiritual attitude toward prayer and repentance as well as toward the practice of the theological virtues. And less emphasis has been put on the repetition of prayer formulas and actions.

5. This *Handbook* first lists the norms for indulgences before listing the different grants of indulgences. These norms are taken either from the apostolic constitution, *Indulgentiarum doctrina*, or from the Code of Canon Law.

It seemed useful for this *Handbook* to give a comprehensive and orderly exposition of all the directives which exist at present concerning indulgences. This was thought especially useful in order to prevent any doubts that may arise in the future concerning this matter.

6. This *Handbook* then first lists three rather broad types of indulgenced grants. These come first to underscore the importance of leading a Christian life day in and day out.

Each of these broader types of grant is followed by some quotations from the scriptures and from the Second Vatican Council. This was done for the benefit and instruction of the faithful to show that each such grant is in harmony with the spirit of the Gospel and with the renewal called forth by the Council.

7. There then follows a listing of grants which concern various specific religious works. The works listed here are indeed few in number since many such works are already included under the broader types of grant mentioned above. In listing specific prayers, it was decided to mention only those prayers which had a somewhat universal appeal and character. Competent church authorities can establish norms for other prayers customarily used in the different rites and places.

8. An appendix has been added to this *Handbook*. It contains a list of invocations and the text of the apostolic constitution *Indulgentiarum doctrina*.

NORMS FOR INDULGENCES

1. An indulgence is the remission in the eyes of God of the temporal punishment due to sins whose culpable element has already been taken away. The Christian faithful who are rightly disposed and observe the definite, prescribed conditions gain this remission through the effective assistance of the Church, which, as the minister of redemption, authoritatively distributes and applies the treasury of the expiatory works of Christ and the saints.[1]

2. An indulgence is either plenary or partial, that is, it frees a person either from all or from some of the temporal punishment due to sins.[2]

3. No one gaining an indulgence may apply it to other living persons.[3]

4. Both partial and plenary indulgences can always be applied to the dead as suffrages.[4]

5. Any of the Christian faithful who, being at least inwardly contrite, perform a work carrying with it a partial indulgence, receive through the Church the remission of temporal punishment equivalent to what their own act already receives.[5]

6. The division of indulgences into "personal," "real," and "local" is no longer used. This is to make it clear that the subject of indulgences is the Christian's act, even though such an act sometimes has a connection with a particular object or place.[6]

7. In addition to the supreme authority of the Church the only ones who can grant indulgences are persons who have this power recognized in law or granted them by the Pope.[7]

---

[1] Apostolic constitution *Indulgentiarum doctrina*, norm 1. See below, p. 118.
[2] Ibid., norm 2.
[3] Cf. 1983 Code of Canon Law, canon 994.
[4] Apostolic constitution *Indulgentiarum doctrina*, norm 3.
[5] Ibid., norm 5.
[6] Ibid., norm 12.
[7] Cf. canon 995.1, C.I.C.

8. In the Roman Curia the Apostolic Penitentiary alone has been put in charge of those matters relating to the granting and use of indulgences. This is without prejudice, however, to the right of the Congregation for the Doctrine of the Faith to oversee whatever involves doctrinal teaching on indulgences.[8]

9. No authority whatsoever below the pope may assign to others the power to grant indulgences, unless such has been expressly granted that authority by the Apostolic See.[9]

10. From the outset of their pastoral office, diocesan bishops and those equivalent to them in law have the right to:

1. grant partial indulgences to the Christian faithful committed to their care;

2. impart the papal blessing with a plenary indulgence, in accord with its prescribed formulary, three times a year in their own dioceses at the end of a Mass which has been celebrated with special liturgical beauty on solemnities or feasts that they will designate, even if they only assist at the Mass.

11. Metropolitans may grant partial indulgences in their suffragan dioceses just as in their own.

12. Patriarchs may grant partial indulgences in every place, even those exempt, of their patriarchate, in churches of their own rite outside the boundaries of their patriarchate, and everywhere in the world for the faithful of their own rite. Archbishops major have the same power.

13. Cardinals possess everywhere the power to grant on particular occasions a partial indulgence which may be gained only by those persons who are present.

14. 1. No book, booklet, or pamphlet listing indulgenced grants is to be published without the permission of the local Ordinary or local Hierarch.

2. The publication, in no matter what language, of an authentic collection of prayers and devotional works to

---

[8] Cf. Apostolic constitution *Regimini Ecclesiae Universae*, 15 August 1967, no. 113 (AAS, 59 [1967]: 923).

[9] Cf. canon 995. 2, C.I.C.

which the Apostolic See has attached indulgences requires the express permission of the same Apostolic See.[10]

15. Those who have obtained from the pope the granting of indulgences in favor of all the faithful are bound by the obligation, under pain of nullification of the favor granted, to send to the Apostolic Penitentiary authentic copies of the concessions given to them.

16. An indulgence attached to any feast is regarded as transferred to the day to which the same feast or its external observance is lawfully transferred.

17. To gain an indulgence attached to a particular day any required visit to a church or oratory may be made from noon of the day preceding until midnight at the end of the assigned day.

18. The Christian faithful gain a partial indulgence in devoutly using religious articles (crucifixes, crosses, rosaries, scapulars, medals) properly blessed by any priest or deacon. But if these religious articles have been blessed by a pope or by any bishop, the faithful devoutly using them may also gain a plenary indulgence on the solemnity of the holy apostles, Peter and Paul, when they add to such use the profession of faith recited in any approved formulary.[11]

19. 1. Indulgences attached to the visiting of a church do not expire if the church is razed and then rebuilt within fifty years on the same or virtually the same site and under the same title.

2. An indulgence attached to the use of a religious article expires only when the article itself ceases to exist or is sold.

20. 1. To be capable of gaining indulgences a person must be baptized, not excommunicated, and in the state of grace at least at the time the prescribed works are completed.

---

[10] Cf. canon 826.3, C.I.C.

[11] Apostolic constitution *Indulgentiarum doctrina,* norm 17.

2. Actually to gain indulgences the person must have at least the general intention of doing so and must perform the acts enjoined at the time stipulated and in the manner required according to the tenor of the grant.[12]

21.   1. A plenary indulgence may be gained only once on any day.

2. A member of the faithful may, however, gain a plenary indulgence at the hour of death even after having gained one already on the same day.

3. A partial indulgence may be gained several times a day, unless something different is explicitly stated.[13]

22.   The prescribed work for gaining a plenary indulgence attached to a church or oratory is a devout visit there, which includes the recitation of the Lord's Prayer and the Creed (*Pater* and *Credo*), unless otherwise stated in a specific grant.[14]

23.   1. Beside the exclusion of all attachment to sin, even venial sin, the requirements for gaining a plenary indulgence are the performance of the indulgenced work and fulfillment of three conditions: sacramental confession, eucharistic communion, and prayer for the pope's intentions.

2. Several plenary indulgences may be gained on the basis of a single sacramental confession; only one may be gained, however, on the basis of a single eucharistic communion and prayer for the pope's intentions.

3. The three conditions may be carried out several days preceding or following performance of the prescribed work. But it is more fitting that the communion and the prayer for the pope's intentions take place on the day the work is performed.

4. If a person is not fully disposed or if the prescribed work and the three mentioned conditions are not fulfilled,

---

[12] Cf. canon 996, C.I.C.

[13] Apostolic constitution *Indulgentiarum doctrina*, norm 6; cf. also norm 18.

[14] Ibid., norm 16.

the indulgence will only be partial; the prescriptions in N. 27 and N. 28 for those impeded are exceptions.

5. The condition requiring prayer for the pope's intentions is satisfied by reciting once the Our Father and Hail Mary for his intentions; nevertheless all the faithful have the option of reciting any other prayer suited to their own piety and devotion.[15]

24. An indulgence cannot be attached to a work to which a person is obliged by law or precept, unless expressly stated in the grant. Nevertheless a person who performs a work imposed as a penance in confession and which may also be indulgenced can at the one time both satisfy the sacramental penance and gain the indulgence.

25. An indulgence annexed to any prayer may be gained no matter what the language of recitation, provided the accuracy of the translation is supported by a declaration either of the Apostolic Penitentiary or of one of the Ordinaries or Hierarchs in the region where the language of the translation is in general use.

26. To gain indulgences it suffices to recite the prayer alternating with another person or to follow it mentally as another recites it.

27. Confessors are empowered to commute either the prescribed work or the necessary conditions in favor of those for whom these are impossible because of some legitimate obstacle.

28. Local Ordinaries or Hierarchs may also grant to the faithful subject to them, in keeping with canon law, and who reside in places where they cannot go to confession or communion at all or can do so only with great hardship that they may gain a plenary indulgence without actual confession and communion, provided they have inner contrition and the resolution to go to these sacraments as soon as possible.[16]

---

[15] Cf. Apostolic constitution *Indulgentiarum doctrina*, norms 7, 8, 9, 10.
[16] Cf ibid., norm 11.

29. The hearing-impaired and the speech-impaired can gain the indulgences attached to public prayers simply by raising their minds and devotion to God as they are present with others of the faithful praying in the same place. In the case of private prayers it is enough for them to go over them mentally and express them in some sign or even simply to read them without pronouncing the words.

THREE GENERAL TYPES OF INDULGENCED GRANTS

PRELIMINARY COMMENTS

1. These three general types of indulgenced grants have for their purpose to encourage the Christian faithful to structure into the texture of their everyday activities a Christian spirit[1] and to gear their lives toward the perfection of charity.[2]

2. The first and second types of grant are more or less the same as many characteristic ones of the past. But the third type of grant is much more in harmony with our own times. For there is more advantage today to encourage the faithful to carry out penitential practices on their own initiative in addition to the actual law of abstinence from meat and the law of fasting—both of which are today rather mitigated.[3]

3. These three types of grant are really rather broad, and each one of them concerns many works of the same generic type. Nevertheless, not all such works are endowed with indulgences but only those which are carried out in a special manner and spirit.

For the sake of example, let us consider the first type of grant which is described as follows: "A partial indulgence is granted to the Christian faithful who, while performing their duties and enduring the difficulties of life, raise their minds in humble trust to God and make, at least mentally, some pious invocation."

In this first type of grant an indulgence is attached only to those acts in which the Christian faithful raise up their minds to God as described above while they perform their duties and put up with the difficulties of life.

---

[1] Cf. 1 Cor 10:31 and Col 3:17; Second Vatican Council, Decree on the Apostolate of the Laity *Apostolicam actuositatem,* nos. 2, 3, 4, and 13.

[2] Cf. Second Vatican Council, Dogmatic Constitution on the Church *Lumen gentium,* no. 39 and nos. 40-42.

[3] Cf. Apostolic Constitution *Paenitemini,* 17 February 1966, III c (AAS, 58 [1966]: 182-183).

Owing to human weakness, however, such special acts are not very frequent. But when a person is so conscientious and devout that he/she performs acts of this type several times during the day, then in addition to a fuller increase of grace he/she rightly obtains a fuller remission of punishment and can in charity render abundant assistance to the souls in purgatory.

These same comments can be made in substance concerning the other two general types of grants.

4. It is obvious that the three types of grant are in special harmony with the gospels and with the teaching of the Church as amply set forth in the Second Vatican Council. For this reason and for the benefit of the faithful citations taken from the scriptures and from the documents of this Council are given below for each of these general types.

THE GRANTS

I

A partial indulgence is granted to the Christian faithful who, while performing their duties and enduring the difficulties of life, raise their minds in humble trust to God and make, at least mentally, some pious invocation.

This type of grant intends to assist the Christian faithful in fulfilling the command of Christ: "You need to pray always and not stop."[4] It also admonishes them to carry out their duties in such a way that they maintain and increase their union with Christ.

Mt 7:7-8: Ask and it will be given to you; seek and you will find; knock and the door will be opened to you. For everyone who asks, receives; and the one who seeks, finds; and to the one who knocks, the door will be opened.

Mt 26:41: Watch and pray that you may not undergo the test.

Lk 21:34-36: Beware that your hearts do not become drowsy from carousing and drunkenness and the anxieties of daily life, and that day catch you by surprise like a trap. For that day will assault everyone who lives on the face of the earth. Be vigilant at all times and pray that you have the strength to escape the tribulations that are imminent and to stand before the Son of Man.

Acts 2:42: They devoted themselves to the teaching of the apostles and to the communal life, to the breaking of the bread and to the prayers.

Rom 12:12: Rejoice in hope, endure in affliction, persevere in prayer.

1 Cor 10:31: So whether you eat or drink, or whatever you do, do everything for the glory of God.

---

[4] Lk 18:1.

Eph 6:18: With all prayer and supplication, pray at every opportunity in the Spirit. To that end, be watchful with all perseverance and supplication for all the holy ones.

Col 3:17: And whatever you do, in word or in deed, do everything in the name of the Lord Jesus, giving thanks to God the Father through him.

Col 4:2: Persevere in prayer, being watchful in it with thanksgiving.

1 Thes 5:17-18: Pray without ceasing. In all circumstances give thanks, for this is the will of God for you in Christ Jesus.

Vatican Council II, Dogmatic Constitution on the Church *Lumen Gentium*, no. 41: Accordingly all Christians, in the conditions, duties and circumstances of their life and through all these, will sanctify themselves more and more if they receive all things with faith from the hand of the heavenly Father and cooperate with the divine will, thus showing forth in that temporal service the love with which God has loved the world.

Vatican Council II, Decree on the Apostolate of Lay People *Apostolicam Actuositatem*, no. 4: This life of intimate union with Christ in the Church is maintained by the spiritual helps common to all the faithful. . . . Lay people should make such a use of these helps that, while meeting their human obligations in the ordinary conditions of life, they do not separate their union with Christ from their ordinary life; but through the very performance of their tasks, which are God's will for them, actually promote the growth of their union with him. . . . Family cares should not be foreign to their spirituality, nor any other temporal interest; in the words of the apostle: "Whatever you do, in word or in deed, do everything in the name of the Lord Jesus, giving thanks to God the Father through him."[5]

---

[5] Col 3:17.

Vatican Council II, Pastoral Constitution on the Church in the Modern World *Gaudium et Spes,* no. 43: One of the gravest errors of our time is the dichotomy between the faith which many profess and the practice of their daily lives. . . . Let there, then, be no such pernicious opposition between professional and social activity on the one hand and religious life on the other. . . . Let Christians follow the example of Christ who worked as a craftsman; let them be proud of the opportunity to carry out their earthly activity in such a way as to integrate human, domestic, professional, scientific and technical enterprises with religious values, under whose supreme direction all things are ordered to the glory of God.

II

A partial indulgence is granted to the Christian faithful who, prompted by a spirit of faith, devote themselves or their goods in compassionate service to their brothers and sisters in need.

This second type of grant intends to induce the Christian faithful to follow the example and the command of Christ Jesus[6] by frequently performing works of charity and mercy.

But this indulgence is not attached to all works of charity. It is attached only to those works done "in compassionate service to their brothers and sisters in need," e.g., persons who are in need of food or clothing for the body or in need of instruction or comfort for their spirits.

---

6 Jn 13:15 and Acts 10:38.

Mt 25:35-36, 40: For I was hungry and you gave me food, I was thirsty and you gave me drink, a stranger and you welcomed me, naked and you clothed me, ill and you cared for me, in prison and you visited me. . . . Amen, I say to you, whatever you did for one of these least brothers of mine, you did it for me.[7]

Jn 13:34-35: I give you a new commandment: love one another. As I have loved you, so you also should love one another. This is how all will know that you are my disciples, if you have love for one another.

Rom 12:8, 10-11, 13: If one exhorts, in exhortation; if one contributes, in generosity; if one is over others, with diligence; if one does acts of mercy, with cheerfulness. . . . Love one another with mutual affection; anticipate one another in showing honor. Do not grow slack in zeal, be fervent in spirit, serve the Lord. . . . Contribute to the needs of the holy ones, exercise hospitality.

1 Cor 13:3: If I give away everything I own, . . . but do not have love, I gain nothing.

Gal 6:10: While we have the opportunity, let us do good to all, but especially to those who belong to the family of the faith.

Eph 5:2: Live in love, as Christ loved us.

1 Thes 4:9: You yourselves have been taught by God to love one another.

Heb 13:1: Let mutual love continue.

Jas 1:27: Religion that is pure and undefiled before God and the Father is this: to care for orphans and widows in their affliction and to keep oneself unstained by the world.[8]

1 Pt 1:22: Since you have purified yourselves by obedience to the truth for sincere mutual love, love one another intensely from a pure heart.

---

[6] Cf. Jn 13:15 and Acts 10:38.
[7] Cf. also Tb 4:7-8 and Is 58:7.

1 Pt 3:8-9: Finally, all of you, be of one mind, sympathetic, loving toward one another, compassionate, humble. Do not return evil for evil, or insult for insult; but, on the contrary, a blessing, because to this you were called, that you might inherit a blessing.

2 Pt 1:5, 7: Make every effort to supplement your . . . devotion with mutual affection, mutual affection with love.

1 Jn 3:17-18: If someone who has worldly means sees a brother in need and refuses him compassion, how can the love of God remain in him? Children, let us love not in word or speech but in deed and truth.

Vatican Council II, Decree on the Apostolate of Lay People *Apostolicam Actuositatem,* no. 8: Wherever people are to be found who are in want of food and drink, of clothing, housing, medicine, work, education, the means necessary for leading a truly human life, wherever there are people racked by misfortune or illness, people suffering exile or imprisonment, Christian charity should go in search of them and find them out, comfort them with devoted care and give them the helps that will relieve their needs. . . . If this exercise of charity is to be above all criticism, and seen to be so, one should see in one's neighbors the image of God to which they have been created, and Christ the Lord to whom is really offered all that is given to the needy.

Ibid., no. 31 c: Works of charity and mercy bear a most striking testimony to Christian life; therefore, an apostolic training which has as its object the performance of these works should enable the faithful to learn from very childhood how to sympathize with their brothers and sisters, and help them generously when in need.

Vatican Council II, Pastoral Constitution on the Church in the Modern World *Gaudium et spes,* conclusion, no. 93: Mindful of the words of the Lord: "This is how all will know that you are my disciples, if you have love for one another,"[9] Christians can yearn for nothing more ardently than to

---

[8] Cf. Jas 2:15-16.
[9] Jn 13:35.

serve the people of this age with an ever growing generosity and success. . . . It is the Father's will that we should recognize Christ our brother in the persons of all people and love them with an effective love, in word and in deed.

III

A partial indulgence is granted to the Christian faithful who, in a spirit of penitence, voluntarily abstain from something which is licit for and pleasing to them.

This third type of grant intends to urge the Christian faithful to hold their appetites in check and thus learn to obtain mastery over their bodies and conform themselves to the poor and suffering Christ.[10]

The excellence of self-control indeed stands out more when it is combined with charity, as St. Leo the Great writes: "We should spend on virtue what we take away from our pleasures. Thus through the abstinence of the fasting person relief may come to the poor."[11]

Lk 9:23: If anyone wishes to come after me, he must deny himself and take up his cross daily and follow me.[12]

Lk 13:5: If you do not repent, you will all perish as they did (cf. ibid. v. 3).

Rom 8:13: If by the spirit you put to death the deeds of the body, you will live.

Rom 8:17: If only we suffer with him so that we may also be glorified with him.

---

[10] Cf. Mt 8:20 and 16:24.

[11] Sermon 13 (sometimes referred to as Sermon 12), *De ieiunio decimi mensis,* 2: PL 54:172.

[12] Cf. Lk 14:27.

1 Cor 9:25-27: Every athlete exercises discipline in every way. They do it to win a perishable crown, but we an imperishable one. Thus I do not run aimlessly; I do not fight as if I were shadowboxing. No. I drive my body and train it.

2 Cor 4:10: Always carrying about in the body the dying of Jesus, so that the life of Jesus may also be manifested in our body.

2 Tm 2:11-12: This saying is trustworthy: If we have died with him we shall also live with him; if we persevere we shall also reign with him.

Ti 2:12: [Rejecting] worldly desires [we should] live temperately, justly, and devoutly in this age.

1 Pt 4:13: But rejoice to the extent that you share in the sufferings of Christ, so that when his glory is revealed you may also rejoice exultantly.

Vatican Council II, Decree on the Training of Priests *Optatam totius,* no. 9: With special care they should be so trained in priestly obedience, poverty and a spirit of self-denial, that they may accustom themselves to living in conformity with the crucified Christ and to giving up willingly even those things which are lawful.

Vatican Council II, Dogmatic Constitution on the Church *Lumen Gentium,* no. 10: The faithful indeed, by virtue of their royal priesthood, participate in the offering of the Eucharist. They exercise that priesthood, too, by the reception of the sacraments, prayer and thanksgiving, the witness of a holy life, abnegation and active charity.

Vatican Council II, Dogmatic Constitution on the Church *Lumen Gentium,* no. 41: The forms and tasks of life are many but holiness is one—that sanctity which is cultivated by all who act under God's Spirit and, obeying the Father's voice and adoring God the Father in spirit and truth, follow Christ, poor, humble and cross-bearing, that they may deserve to be partakers of his glory.

Apostolic Constitution on Christian Penance *Paenitemini, III, c:* The Church nevertheless appeals to all the faithful together that they obey the Lord's command to repent not only through the hardships and setbacks bound up with the nature of daily life, but also by acts of bodily mortification. . . .

The Church is intent especially upon expressing the three principal ways, longstanding in its practice, which make it possible to fulfill the divine command to repent. These are prayer, fasting, and works of charity—even though fast and abstinence have had a privileged place. These ways of penance have been shared by all the centuries; yet in our own time there are particular reasons advanced in favor of one way of penance above the others, depending on circumstances. For example, in the richer nations stress is placed on the witness of self-denial so that Christians will not become worldly; another emphasis is the witness of charity toward others, even those in foreign lands, who are suffering poverty and hunger.[13]

---

[13] AAS, 58 [1966]: 182-183 [DOL 358, nos. 3019-3020].

THE OTHER TYPES OF INDULGENCED GRANTS

PRELIMINARY COMMENTS

1. A few more types of indulgenced grants are here added to the three general types listed above in I-III. These other types exhibit a distinctive character of their own since they take into consideration the traditions of the past as well as the concerns of our own times.

All these other types of grant complement one another. In offering the gift of an indulgence they intend to lead the Christian faithful to perform works of devotion, charity, and penitence and to lead them by means of charity to closer union with the body of the Church and with Christ, its head.[1]

2. Certain prayers are listed in this section. These prayers merit great respect owing to their divine inspiration or their antiquity and upon their more or less universal usage, e.g., the *Creed* (no. 16); the *De Profundis* (no. 19); the *Magnificat* (no. 30); the Ancient Prayer to Mary (no. 57); the Hail, Holy Queen (no. 51); the Prayer for All Occasions (no. 1); and the Prayer of Thanksgiving (no. 7).

Upon close inspection it becomes obvious that these prayers are already included in the first general type of grant. For these prayers are recited in the course of their everyday lives by the Christian faithful with hearts raised in humble trust to God.

As examples of such overlapping with the first general type we can mention the Prayer for All Occasions and the Prayer of Thanksgiving, since they are recited during the course of "carrying out one's duties."

---

[1] Cf. Apostolic constitution *Indulgentiarum doctrina*, no. 11.

But it seemed helpful to list these prayers separately as being endowed with indulgences in order to eliminate any doubt and to indicate their prominence.

3. In this section are also found individual works to which an indulgence is attached. The grant of a partial indulgence is sometimes expressly stated and explained; but often it is indicated only by the rubric: partial indulgence.

When some work is endowed with a plenary indulgence owing to special circumstances, the plenary grant and the special circumstances which define the work in detail are expressly noted for each and every such grant. For the sake of brevity, the other types of works endowed with indulgences are not so noted; and it is to be understood that the indulgence attached to these works is a partial one.

As stated in norm 23, the requirements for obtaining a plenary indulgence are: the execution of the work, the fulfillment of the three conditions, and that full disposition of spirit which excludes all attachment to sin.

4. When the work to which a plenary indulgence is attached can easily be divided into parts (e.g., the division of the Marian Rosary into decades), a person who owing to some reasonable cause cannot complete the entire work can obtain a partial indulgence for that part which was completed.

5. Worth special mention are those grants which list works by which the Christian faithful, by performing any one of them, can obtain a plenary indulgence every day of the year:

— adoration of the Blessed Sacrament for at least one half hour (no. 3);

— devout reading of the Sacred Scriptures for at least one half hour (no. 50);

— the devout performance of the Stations of the Cross (no. 63);

— the recitation of the Marian Rosary in a church or oratory, with members of the family, in a religious Community, or in a pious association (no. 48).

But even in these instances what is stated in norm 21, paragraph 1, retains its force, namely, a plenary indulgence can be obtained but once a day.

The following grants are listed in alphabetical order. This arrangement is based on the following: in the case of the prayers, the first words of the (Latin) *text of each prayer is listed (e.g., Agimus tibi gratias; Angelus Domini); in the case of the works, the first words by which the work itself is known in Latin is listed (e.g., Viae Crucis exercitium [Stations of the Cross, performance of]; Votorum baptismalium renovatio [Vows of Baptism, renewal of]).*

THE GRANTS

1

Actiones nostras

Prayer for All Occasions

Lord,
may everything we do
begin with your inspiration
and continue with your help,
so that all our prayers and works
may begin in you
and by you be happily ended.

We ask this through Christ our Lord.
Amen.

> (Roman Missal, Thursday after Ash Wednesday, Opening
> Prayer; The Liturgy of the Hours, Week I, Monday, Morning
> Prayer.)

A partial indulgence.

2

Actus virtutum theologalium et contritionis

Act of Faith, Hope, and Love and Act of Contrition

A *partial indulgence* is granted the Christian faithful
when they devoutly recite in any legitimate formula acts of
faith, hope, and charity and an act of contrition which is
joined to them. The individual acts are each endowed with
the indulgence.

Act of Faith, Hope, and Love

My God, I believe in you,
I trust in you,
I love you above all things,
with all my heart and mind and strength.
I love you because you are supremely good and worth
    loving;
and because I love you,
I am sorry with all my heart for offending you.
Lord, have mercy on me, a sinner.
Amen.

Act of Contrition

My God,
I am sorry for my sins with all my heart.
In choosing to do wrong
and failing to do good,
I have sinned against you
whom I should love above all things.
I firmly intend, with your help,
to do penance,
to sin no more,
and to avoid whatever leads me to sin.

Our Savior Jesus Christ
suffered and died for us.
In his name, my God, have mercy.

3

Adoratio Ss.mi Sacramenti

Adoration of the Blessed Sacrament

A *partial indulgence* is granted the Christian faithful
when they visit the Blessed Sacrament for the purpose of
adoration. When this is done for at least half an hour, the
indulgence is a plenary one.

4

Adoro te devote

Hidden Here before Me, Lord

Hidden here before me, Lord, I worship you,
Hidden in these symbols, yet completely true.
Lord, my soul surrenders, longing to obey,
And in contemplation wholly faints away.

Seeing, touching, tasting: these are all deceived;
Only through the hearing can it be believed.
Nothing is more certain: Christ has told me so;
What the Truth has uttered, I believe and know.

Only God was hidden when you came to die:
Human nature also here escapes the eye.
Both are my profession, both are my belief:
Bring me to your Kingdom, like the dying thief.

I am not like Thomas, who could see and touch;
Though your wounds are hidden, I believe as much.
Let me say so boldly, meaning what I say,
Loving you and trusting, now and every day.

Record of the Passion when the Lamb was slain,
Living bread that brings us back to life again:
Feed me with your presence, make me live on you;
Let that lovely fragrance fill me through and through.

Once a nesting pelican gashed herself to blood
For the preservation of her starving brood:
Now heal me with your blood, take away my guilt:
All the world is ransomed if one drop is spilt.

Jesus, for the present seen as through a mask,
Give me what I thirst for, give me what I ask:
Let me see your glory in a blaze of light,
And instead of blindness give me, Lord, my sight. Amen.

A *partial indulgence* is granted the Christian faithful
who devoutly recite the poem, Adoro te.

5

Adsumus

Prayer for Meetings

We stand before you, Holy Spirit,
conscious of our sinfulness,
but aware that we gather in your name.

Come to us, remain with us,
and enlighten our hearts.

Give us light and strength
to know your will,
to make it our own,
and to live it in our lives.

Guide us by your wisdom,
support us by your power,
for you are God,
sharing the glory of Father and Son.

You desire justice for all:
enable us to uphold the rights of others;
do not allow us to be misled by ignorance
or corrupted by fear or favor.

Unite us to yourself in the bond of love
and keep us faithful to all that is true.

As we gather in your name
may we temper justice with love,
so that all our decisions
may be pleasing to you,
and earn the reward
promised to good and faithful servants.
Amen.

This prayer, which is usually recited before meetings dealing with common concerns, is endowed with a *partial indulgence*.

6

Ad te, beate Ioseph

Prayer to Saint Joseph

Blessed Joseph, husband of Mary, be with us this day.
You protected and cherished the Virgin;
loving the Child Jesus as your Son,
you rescued him from danger of death.
Defend the Church, the household of God,
purchased by the blood of Christ.

Guardian of the holy family,
be with us in our trials.
May your prayers obtain for us
the strength to flee from error
and wrestle with the powers of corruption
so that in life we may grow in holiness
and in death rejoice in the crown of victory.
Amen.

A partial indulgence.

7

Agimus tibi gratias

Prayer of Thanksgiving

We give you thanks
for all your gifts,
almighty God,
living and reigning
now and for ever.
Amen.

A partial indulgence.

8

Angele Dei

Prayer to the Guardian Angel

Angel sent by God to guide me,
be my light and walk beside me;
be my guardian and protect me;
on the paths of life direct me.

A partial indulgence.

9

Angelus Domini et Regina caeli

The Angelus and the Regina Caeli

a) *Throughout the year:*

℣. The angel spoke God's message to Mary,
℟. *and she conceived of the Holy Spirit.*
Hail, Mary . . .

℣. "I am the lowly servant of the Lord:
℟. *let it be done to me according to your word."*
Hail, Mary . . .

℣. And the Word became flesh
℟. *and lived among us.*
Hail, Mary . . .

℣. Pray for us, holy Mother of God,
℟. *that we may become worthy of the promises of Christ.*

Let us pray.

Lord,
fill our hearts with your grace:
once, through the message of an angel
you revealed to us the incarnation of your Son;
now, through his suffering and death
lead us to the glory of his resurrection.

We ask this through Christ our Lord.

℟. *Amen.*

> (Roman Missal, Fourth Sunday of Advent, Opening Prayer.)

b) *During the Season of Easter:*

Queen of heaven, rejoice, alleluia.
  For Christ, your Son and Son of God,
  has risen as he said, alleluia.
  Pray to God for us, alleluia.

℣. Rejoice and be glad, O Virgin Mary, alleluia.
℟. *For the Lord has truly risen, alleluia.*

> (Cf. The Liturgy of the Hours, Season of Easter, after Night Prayer.)

Let us pray.

God of life,
you have given joy to the world
by the resurrection of your Son, our Lord Jesus Christ.
Through the prayers of his mother, the Virgin Mary,
bring us to the happiness of eternal life.

We ask this through Christ our Lord.
℟. *Amen.*

> (Roman Missal, Common of the Blessed Virgin Mary, Season of Easter, Opening Prayer.)

A *partial indulgence* is granted the Christian faithful who devoutly recite these prayers during the times stated. According to a praiseworthy custom these prayers are usually recited at dawn, noon, and in the evening.

10

Anima Christi

Soul of Christ

Soul of Christ, sanctify me.
Body of Christ, heal me.
Blood of Christ, drench me.
Water from the side of Christ, wash me.
Passion of Christ, strengthen me.

Good Jesus, hear me.

In your wounds shelter me.
From turning away keep me.
From the evil one protect me.
At the hour of my death call me.
Into your presence lead me,
to praise you with all your saints
for ever and ever.
Amen.

> (Roman Missal, p. 935.)

A partial indulgence.

11

Basilicarum Patriarchalium in Urbe visitatio

Visiting the Patriarchal Basilicas in Rome

A *plenary indulgence* is granted the Christian faithful who devoutly visit one of the four patriarchal basilicas in Rome and there recite the Our Father and the Creed:

1) on the basilica's titular feast;
2) on Sundays and the other 10 holy days of obligation;[2]
3) once a year on any other day chosen by the individual Christian faithful.

---

[2] Cf. *Code of Canon Law*, canon 1246, paragraph 1.

12

Benedictio Papalis

Papal Blessing

A *plenary indulgence* is granted the Christian faithful who devoutly receive the blessing imparted either by the Roman Pontiff to the City and to the World or by a bishop to the faithful entrusted to his care in accord with norm number 10, paragraph 2, of this *Handbook*. This grant extends also to such blessings when given by means of radio or television.

13

Coemeterii visitatio

Visiting a Cemetery

An indulgence is granted the Christian faithful who devoutly visit a cemetery and pray, if only mentally, for the dead. This indulgence is applicable only to the souls in purgatory. This indulgence is a *plenary* one from November 1 through November 8 and can be gained on each one of these days. On the other days of the year this indulgence is a *partial* one.

14

Coemeterii veterum christianorum
seu "catacumbae" visitatio

Visiting a Catacomb, i.e., a Cemetery of the Early Christians

A *partial indulgence* is granted the Christian faithful who devoutly visit a "catacomb," i.e., a cemetery of the early Christians.

15

Communionis spiritalis actus

Act of Spiritual Communion

An act of spiritual communion, expressed in any devout formula whatsoever, is endowed with a *partial indulgence.*

16

Creo in Deum

Creed

Apostles' Creed

I believe in God,
the Father almighty,
Creator of heaven and earth,
and in Jesus Christ, his only Son, our Lord,
who was conceived by the Holy Spirit,
born of the Virgin Mary,
suffered under Pontius Pilate,
was crucified, died and was buried;
he descended into hell;
on the third day he rose again from the dead;
he ascended into heaven,
and is seated at the right hand of God the Father almighty;
from there he will come to judge the living and the dead.

I believe in the Holy Spirit,
the holy catholic Church,
the communion of saints,
the forgiveness of sins,
the resurrection of the body,
and life everlasting. Amen.

Niceno-Constantinopolitan Creed

I believe in one God,
the Father almighty,
maker of heaven and earth,
of all things visible and invisible.

I believe in one Lord Jesus Christ,
the Only Begotten Son of God,
born of the Father before all ages.
God from God, Light from Light,
true God from true God,
begotten, not made, consubstantial with the Father;
through him all things were made.
For us men and for our salvation
he came down from heaven,
and by the Holy Spirit was incarnate of the Virgin Mary,
and became man.

For our sake he was crucified under Pontius Pilate,
he suffered death and was buried,
and rose again on the third day
in accordance with the Scriptures.
He ascended into heaven
and is seated at the right hand of the Father.
He will come again in glory
to judge the living and the dead
and his kingdom will have no end.

I believe in the Holy Spirit, the Lord, the giver of life,
who proceeds from the Father and the Son,
who with the Father and the Son is adored and glorified,
who has spoken through the prophets.

I believe in one, holy, catholic and apostolic Church.
I confess one Baptism for the forgiveness of sins
and I look forward to the resurrection of the dead
and the life of the world to come. Amen.

A *partial indulgence* is granted the Christian faithful who devoutly recite the above Apostles' Creed or the Niceno-Constantinopolitan Creed.

17

Crucis adoratio

Adoration of the Cross

A *plenary indulgence* is granted the Christian faithful who devoutly take part in the adoration of the cross during the solemn liturgy of Good Friday.

18

Defunctorum officium

Office for the Dead

A *partial indulgence* is granted the Christian faithful who devoutly recite Morning Prayer or Evening Prayer from the Office for the Dead.

19

De profundis

Psalm 130

A *partial indulgence* is granted the Christian faithful who devoutly recite Psalm 130, the *De Profundis* (Out of the depths I cry to you, O Lord).

Out of the depths I call to you, Lord;
Lord, hear my cry!
May your ears be attentive
to my cry for mercy.

If you, Lord, mark our sins,
Lord, who can stand?
But with you is forgiveness
and so you are revered.

I wait with longing for the Lord,
my soul waits for his word.
My soul looks for the Lord
more than sentinels for daybreak.

More than sentinels for daybreak,
let Israel look for the Lord,
For with the Lord is kindness,
with him is full redemption,
And God will redeem Israel
from all their sins.

[Glory to the Father, and to the Son, and to the Holy Spirit:
as it was in the beginning, is now, and will be for ever.
Amen.]

20

Doctrina christiana

Teaching or Studying Christian Doctrine

A *partial indulgence* is granted the Christian faithful
who either teach or study Christian doctrine.

N.B.—A person who teaches Christian doctrine
prompted by a spirit of faith and charity can acquire a
partial indulgence in accord with the second general type of
indulgenced grant mentioned on page 29.

This present grant, number 20, restates the *partial indulgence* as regards the teacher but extends it also to include the person who studies Christian doctrine.

21

Domine, Deus omnipotens

Prayer at the Beginning of the Day

Almighty God,
you have given us this day:
strengthen us with your power
and keep us from falling into sin,
so that whatever we say or think or do
may be in your service and for the sake of your kingdom.

We ask this through Christ our Lord.
Amen.

A *partial indulgence.*

22

En ego, o bone et dulcissime Iesu

Prayer before a Crucifix

Good and gentle Jesus,
I kneel before you.
I see and I ponder your five wounds.
My eyes behold what David prophesied about you:
"They have pierced my hands and feet;
they have counted all my bones."

Engrave on me this image of yourself.
Fulfill the yearnings of my heart:
give me faith, hope, and love,
repentance for my sins,
and true conversion of life.
Amen.

(Psalm 22:17-18; Roman Missal, pp. 935-936.)

On any Friday during Lent a *plenary indulgence* is granted the Christian faithful who, after communion, devoutly recite the above prayer before an image of Jesus Christ crucified. On other days of the year the indulgence is a *partial* one.

23

Eucharisticus conventus

Eucharistic Congresses

A *plenary indulgence* is granted the Christian faithful who devoutly participate in the solemn eucharistic rite which customarily closes a eucharistic congress.

24

Exaudi nos

Prayer for the Household

Hear us, Lord,
and send your angel from heaven
to visit and protect,
to comfort and defend
all who live in this house.
Amen.

A *partial indulgence.*

25

Exercitia spiritalia

Retreats

A *plenary indulgence* is granted the Christian faithful who spend at least three full days of spiritual exercises during a retreat.

26

Iesu dulcissime

Act of Reparation to the Sacred Heart

Most loving Jesus,
how great is the love which you have poured out upon the
world.
How casual and careless is our response!
Kneeling before you, we wish to atone
for the indifference and the slights which pierce you to the
heart.

℟. *Praise to the heart of Jesus, our Savior and our God.*

We ask forgiveness for our own shameful neglect.
We wish to make amends
for those who are obstinate in their unbelief,
for those who turn away from the light
and wander like sheep without a shepherd;
and for those who have broken their baptismal promises
and reject the gentle yoke of your law.

℟. *Praise to the heart of Jesus, our Savior and our God.*

We wish to make amends for the sins of our society:
for lust and degradation,
for the corruption of the young,
for indifference and blasphemy,
for attacks against your Church,
for irreverence and even sacrilege
against your love in this blessed sacrament,
and for the public defiance of your law.

℟. *Praise to the heart of Jesus, our Savior and our God.*

These are the sins for which you died,
but now we share in your atonement
by offering on the altar in union with you
the living sacrifice you made on the cross,
joining to it the sufferings of your Virgin Mother,
and those of all the saints and the whole Church.

R̝. *Praise to the heart of Jesus, our Savior and our God.*

We promise faithfully
that by your grace
we shall make reparation for our own sins
and for those of others
by a strong faith,
by holy living,
and by obedience to the law of the Gospel,
whose greatest commandment is that of charity.

R̝. *Praise to the heart of Jesus, our Savior and our God.*

We also promise to do our best
to discourage others from insulting you
and bring those we can to follow you.

R̝. *Praise to the heart of Jesus, our Savior and our God.*

Jesus, Lord,
receive this loving act of homage
together with the prayers of our Lady,
who stood by the cross,
our model in reparation.
Keep us faithful, even to the point of death,
give us the gift of perseverance
and lead us all to our promised land in heaven,
where you, with the Father and the Holy Spirit,
live and reign for ever and ever. Amen.

R̝. *Praise to the heart of Jesus, our Savior and our God.*

A *partial indulgence* is granted the Christian faithful who devoutly recite the above act of reparation. This indulgence will be a *plenary* one when this Act of Reparation is publicly recited on the solemnity of the Sacred Heart of Jesus.

27

Iesu dulcissime, Redemptor

Act of Dedication to Christ the King

Loving Jesus, Redeemer of the world,
we are yours, and yours we wish to be.
To bind ourselves to you even more closely
we kneel before you today
and offer ourselves to your most Sacred Heart.

℟. *Praise to you, our Savior and our King.*

Have mercy on all who have never known you
and on all who reject you and refuse to obey you:
gentle Lord, draw them to yourself.

℟. *Praise to you, our Savior and our King.*

Reign over the faithful who have never left you,
reign over those who have squandered their inheritance,
the prodigal children who now are starving:
bring them back to their Father's house.

℟. *Praise to you, our Savior and our King.*

Reign over those who are misled by error or divided by
discord.
Hasten the day when we shall be one in faith and truth,
one flock with you, the one Shepherd.
Give to your Church freedom and peace,
and to all nations justice and order.
Make the earth resound from pole to pole with a single cry:
Praise to the Divine Heart that gained our salvation;
glory and honor be his for ever and ever. Amen.

℟. *Praise to you, our Savior and our King.*

A *partial indulgence* is granted the Christian faithful
who devoutly recite the above Act of Dedication to Christ
the King. This indulgence will be a *plenary* one when this
Act is publicly recited on the solemnity of our Lord, Jesus
Christ, the King.

28

In articulo mortis

At the Approach of Death

Priests who minister the sacraments to the Christian faithful who are in a life-and-death situation should not neglect to impart to them the apostolic blessing, with its attached indulgence. But if a priest cannot be present, holy mother Church lovingly grants such persons who are rightly disposed a *plenary indulgence* to be obtained *in articulo mortis,* at the approach of death, provided they regularly prayed in some way during their lifetime. The use of a crucifix or a cross is recommended in obtaining this plenary indulgence.

In such a situation the three usual conditions required in order to gain a plenary indulgence are substituted for by the condition "provided they regularly prayed in some way."

The Christian faithful can obtain the plenary indulgence mentioned here as death approaches (*in articulo mortis*) even if they had already obtained another plenary indulgence that same day.

This grant, number 28, is taken from the apostolic constitution *Indulgentiarum doctrina,* norm 18.

29

Litaniae

Litanies

A *partial indulgence* is attached to each of those litanies which have been approved by competent authority. The following litanies are recommended as standing out from all the others: Litany of the Holy Name; Litany of the Sacred Heart; Litany of the Precious Blood; Litany of the Blessed Virgin Mary; Litany of Saint Joseph; and the Litany of the Saints. (Translations are provided below.)

Litany of the Holy Name

Lord, have mercy — *Lord, have mercy*
Christ, have mercy — *Christ, have mercy*
Lord, have mercy — *Lord, have mercy*

God our Father in heaven — *have mercy on us*
God the Son, Redeemer of the world — *have mercy on us*
God the Holy Spirit — *have mercy on us*
Holy Trinity, one God — *have mercy on us*

Jesus, Son of the living God — *have mercy on us*
Jesus, splendor of the Father — *have mercy on us*
Jesus, brightness of everlasting light — *have mercy on us*
Jesus, king of glory — *have mercy on us*
Jesus, dawn of justice — *have mercy on us*
Jesus, Son of the Virgin Mary — *have mercy on us*
Jesus, worthy of our love — *have mercy on us*
Jesus, worthy of our wonder — *have mercy on us*
Jesus, mighty God — *have mercy on us*
Jesus, father of the world to come — *have mercy on us*
Jesus, prince of peace — *have mercy on us*
Jesus, all-powerful — *have mercy on us*
Jesus, pattern of patience — *have mercy on us*
Jesus, model of obedience — *have mercy on us*
Jesus, gentle and humble of heart — *have mercy on us*

Jesus, lover of chastity — *have mercy on us*
Jesus, lover of us all — *have mercy on us*
Jesus, God of peace — *have mercy on us*
Jesus, author of life — *have mercy on us*
Jesus, model of goodness — *have mercy on us*
Jesus, seeker of souls — *have mercy on us*
Jesus, our God — *have mercy on us*
Jesus, our refuge — *have mercy on us*
Jesus, father of the poor — *have mercy on us*
Jesus, treasure of the faithful — *have mercy on us*

Jesus, Good Shepherd — *have mercy on us*
Jesus, the true light — *have mercy on us*
Jesus, eternal wisdom — *have mercy on us*
Jesus, infinite goodness — *have mercy on us*
Jesus, our way and our life — *have mercy on us*
Jesus, joy of angels — *have mercy on us*
Jesus, king of patriarchs — *have mercy on us*
Jesus, teacher of apostles — *have mercy on us*
Jesus, master of evangelists — *have mercy on us*
Jesus, courage of martyrs — *have mercy on us*

Jesus, light of confessors	*have mercy on us*
Jesus, purity of virgins	*have mercy on us*
Jesus, crown of all saints	*have mercy on us*

Lord, be merciful	*Jesus, save your people*
From all evil	*Jesus, save your people*
From every sin	*Jesus, save your people*
From the snares of the devil	*Jesus, save your people*
From your anger	*Jesus, save your people*
From the spirit of infidelity	*Jesus, save your people*
From everlasting death	*Jesus, save your people*
From neglect of your Holy Spirit	*Jesus, save your people*

By the mystery of your incarnation	*Jesus, save your people*
By your birth	*Jesus, save your people*
By your childhood	*Jesus, save your people*
By your hidden life	*Jesus, save your people*
By your public ministry	*Jesus, save your people*
By your agony and crucifixion	*Jesus, save your people*
By your abandonment	*Jesus, save your people*
By your grief and sorrow	*Jesus, save your people*
By your death and burial	*Jesus, save your people*
By your rising to new life	*Jesus, save your people*
By your return in glory to the Father	*Jesus, save your people*
By your gift of the holy eucharist	*Jesus, save your people*
By your joy and glory	*Jesus, save your people*

Christ, hear us	*Christ, hear us*
Lord Jesus, hear our prayer	*Lord Jesus, hear our prayer*

Lamb of God, you take away the sins of the world	*have mercy on us*
Lamb of God, you take away the sins of the world	*have mercy on us*
Lamb of God, you take away the sins of the world	*have mercy on us*

Let us pray.

Lord,
may we who honor the holy name of Jesus
enjoy his friendship in this life
and be filled with eternal joy in the kingdom
where he lives and reigns for ever and ever.
℟. *Amen.*

Litany of the Sacred Heart

Lord, have mercy	*Lord, have mercy*
Christ, have mercy	*Christ, have mercy*
Lord, have mercy	*Lord, have mercy*
God our Father in heaven	*have mercy on us*
God the Son, Redeemer of the world	*have mercy on us*
God the Holy Spirit	*have mercy on us*
Holy Trinity, one God	*have mercy on us*
Heart of Jesus, Son of the eternal Father	*have mercy on us*
Heart of Jesus, formed by the Holy Spirit in the womb of the Virgin Mother	*have mercy on us*
Heart of Jesus, one with the eternal Word	*have mercy on us*
Heart of Jesus, infinite in majesty	*have mercy on us*
Heart of Jesus, holy temple of God	*have mercy on us*
Heart of Jesus, tabernacle of the Most High	*have mercy on us*
Heart of Jesus, house of God and gate of heaven	*have mercy on us*
Heart of Jesus, aflame with love for us	*have mercy on us*
Heart of Jesus, source of justice and love	*have mercy on us*
Heart of Jesus, full of goodness and love	*have mercy on us*
Heart of Jesus, well-spring of all virtue	*have mercy on us*
Heart of Jesus, worthy of all praise	*have mercy on us*
Heart of Jesus, king and center of all hearts	*have mercy on us*
Heart of Jesus, treasure-house of wisdom and knowledge	*have mercy on us*
Heart of Jesus, in whom there dwells the fullness of God	*have mercy on us*
Heart of Jesus, in whom the Father is well pleased	*have mercy on us*
Heart of Jesus, from whose fullness we have all received	*have mercy on us*
Heart of Jesus, desire of the eternal hills	*have mercy on us*
Heart of Jesus, patient and full of mercy	*have mercy on us*
Heart of Jesus, generous to all who turn to you	*have mercy on us*
Heart of Jesus, fountain of life and holiness	*have mercy on us*
Heart of Jesus, atonement for our sins	*have mercy on us*
Heart of Jesus, overwhelmed with insults	*have mercy on us*
Heart of Jesus, broken for our sins	*have mercy on us*
Heart of Jesus, obedient even to death	*have mercy on us*
Heart of Jesus, pierced by a lance	*have mercy on us*
Heart of Jesus, source of all consolation	*have mercy on us*

Heart of Jesus, our life and resurrection	*have mercy on us*
Heart of Jesus, our peace and reconciliation	*have mercy on us*
Heart of Jesus, victim of our sins	*have mercy on us*
Heart of Jesus, salvation of all who trust in you	*have mercy on us*
Heart of Jesus, hope of all who die in you	*have mercy on us*
Heart of Jesus, delight of all the saints	*have mercy on us*
Lamb of God, you take away the sins of the world	*have mercy on us*
Lamb of God, you take away the sins of the world	*have mercy on us*
Lamb of God, you take away the sins of the world	*have mercy on us*

℣. Jesus, gentle and humble of heart.
℟. *Touch our hearts and make them like your own.*

Let us pray.

Father,
we rejoice in the gifts of love
we have received from the heart of Jesus your Son.
Open our hearts to share his life
and continue to bless us with his love.

We ask this in the name of Jesus the Lord.
℟. *Amen.*

Litany of the Precious Blood

Lord, have mercy	*Lord, have mercy*
Christ, have mercy	*Christ, have mercy*
Lord, have mercy	*Lord, have mercy*
God our Father in heaven	*have mercy on us*
God the Son, Redeemer of the world	*have mercy on us*
God the Holy Spirit	*have mercy on us*
Holy Trinity, one God	*have mercy on us*
Blood of Christ, only Son of the Father	*be our salvation*
Blood of Christ, incarnate Word	*be our salvation*
Blood of Christ, of the new and eternal covenant	*be our salvation*
Blood of Christ, that spilled to the ground	*be our salvation*
Blood of Christ, that flowed at the scourging	*be our salvation*
Blood of Christ, dripping from the thorns	*be our salvation*
Blood of Christ, shed on the cross	*be our salvation*
Blood of Christ, the price of our redemption	*be our salvation*
Blood of Christ, our only claim to pardon	*be our salvation*
Blood of Christ, our blessing cup	*be our salvation*
Blood of Christ, in which we are washed	*be our salvation*
Blood of Christ, torrent of mercy	*be our salvation*
Blood of Christ, that overcomes evil	*be our salvation*
Blood of Christ, strength of the martyrs	*be our salvation*
Blood of Christ, endurance of the saints	*be our salvation*
Blood of Christ, that makes the barren fruitful	*be our salvation*
Blood of Christ, protection of the threatened	*be our salvation*
Blood of Christ, comfort of the weary	*be our salvation*
Blood of Christ, solace of the mourner	*be our salvation*
Blood of Christ, hope of the repentant	*be our salvation*
Blood of Christ, consolation of the dying	*be our salvation*
Blood of Christ, our peace and refreshment	*be our salvation*
Blood of Christ, our pledge of life	*be our salvation*
Blood of Christ, by which we pass to glory	*be our salvation*
Blood of Christ, most worthy of honor	*be our salvation*
Lamb of God, you take away the sins of the world	*have mercy on us*
Lamb of God, you take away the sins of the world	*have mercy on us*
Lamb of God, you take away the sins of the world	*have mercy on us*

℣. Lord, you redeemed us by your blood.
℟. *You have made us a kingdom to serve our God.*

Let us pray.

Father,
by the blood of your Son
you have set us free and saved us from death.
Continue your work of love within us,
that by constantly celebrating the mystery of our salvation
we may reach the eternal life it promises.

We ask this through Christ our Lord.
℟. *Amen.*

Litany of the Blessed Virgin Mary (Litany of Loreto)

Lord, have mercy	*Lord, have mercy*
Christ, have mercy	*Christ, have mercy*
Lord, have mercy	*Lord, have mercy*
God our Father in heaven	*have mercy on us*
God the Son, Redeemer of the world	*have mercy on us*
God the Holy Spirit	*have mercy on us*
Holy Trinity, one God	*have mercy on us*
Holy Mary	*pray for us*
Holy Mother of God	*pray for us*
Most honored of virgins	*pray for us*
Mother of Christ	*pray for us*
Mother of the Church	*pray for us*
Mother of divine grace	*pray for us*
Mother most pure	*pray for us*
Mother of chaste love	*pray for us*
Mother and virgin	*pray for us*
Sinless Mother	*pray for us*
Dearest of mothers	*pray for us*
Model of motherhood	*pray for us*
Mother of good counsel	*pray for us*
Mother of our Creator	*pray for us*
Mother of our Savior	*pray for us*
Virgin most wise	*pray for us*
Virgin rightly praised	*pray for us*
Virgin rightly renowned	*pray for us*
Virgin most powerful	*pray for us*
Virgin gentle in mercy	*pray for us*
Faithful Virgin	*pray for us*
Mirror of justice	*pray for us*
Throne of wisdom	*pray for us*
Cause of our joy	*pray for us*
Shrine of the Spirit	*pray for us*
Glory of Israel	*pray for us*
Vessel of selfless devotion	*pray for us*
Mystical Rose	*pray for us*
Tower of David	*pray for us*
Tower of ivory	*pray for us*
House of gold	*pray for us*
Ark of the covenant	*pray for us*
Gate of heaven	*pray for us*
Morning Star	*pray for us*

Health of the sick	*pray for us*
Refuge of sinners	*pray for us*
Comfort of the troubled	*pray for us*
Help of Christians	*pray for us*
Queen of angels	*pray for us*
Queen of patriarchs and prophets	*pray for us*
Queen of apostles and martyrs	*pray for us*
Queen of confessors and virgins	*pray for us*
Queen of all saints	*pray for us*
Queen conceived without sin	*pray for us*
Queen assumed into heaven	*pray for us*
Queen of the rosary	*pray for us*
Queen of peace	*pray for us*
Lamb of God, you take away the sins of the world	*have mercy on us*
Lamb of God, you take away the sins of the world	*have mercy on us*
Lamb of God, you take away the sins of the world	*have mercy on us*

℣. Pray for us, holy Mother of God.
℟. *That we may become worthy of the promises of Christ.*

Let us pray.

Eternal God,
let your people enjoy constant health in mind and body.
Through the intercession of the Virgin Mary
free us from the sorrows of this life
and lead us to happiness in the life to come.

Grant this through Christ our Lord.
℟. *Amen.*

Litany of Saint Joseph

Lord, have mercy	*Lord, have mercy*
Christ, have mercy	*Christ, have mercy*
Lord, have mercy	*Lord, have mercy*
God our Father in heaven	*have mercy on us*
God the Son, Redeemer of the world	*have mercy on us*
God the Holy Spirit	*have mercy on us*
Holy Trinity, one God	*have mercy on us*
Holy Mary	*pray for us*
Saint Joseph	*pray for us*
Noble son of the House of David	*pray for us*
Light of patriarchs	*pray for us*
Husband of the Mother of God	*pray for us*
Guardian of the Virgin	*pray for us*
Foster father of the Son of God	*pray for us*
Faithful guardian of Christ	*pray for us*
Head of the holy family	*pray for us*
Joseph, chaste and just	*pray for us*
Joseph, prudent and brave	*pray for us*
Joseph, obedient and loyal	*pray for us*
Pattern of patience	*pray for us*
Lover of poverty	*pray for us*
Model of workers	*pray for us*
Example to parents	*pray for us*
Guardian of virgins	*pray for us*
Pillar of family life	*pray for us*
Comfort of the troubled	*pray for us*
Hope of the sick	*pray for us*
Patron of the dying	*pray for us*
Terror of evil spirits	*pray for us*
Protector of the Church	*pray for us*

Lamb of God, you take away
  the sins of the world   *have mercy on us*
Lamb of God, you take away
  the sins of the world   *have mercy on us*
Lamb of God, you take away
  the sins of the world   *have mercy on us*

℣. God made him master of his household.
℟. *And put him in charge of all that he owned.*

Let us pray.

Almighty God,
in your infinite wisdom and love
you chose Joseph to be the husband of Mary,
the mother of your Son.
As we enjoy his protection on earth
may we have the help of his prayers in heaven.

We ask this through Christ our Lord.

℟. *Amen.*

Litany of the Saints

Lord, have mercy	*Lord, have mercy*
Christ, have mercy	*Christ, have mercy*
Lord, have mercy	*Lord, have mercy*

Holy Mary, Mother of God	*pray for us*
Saint Michael	*pray for us*
Holy Angels of God	*pray for us*
Saint John the Baptist	*pray for us*
Saint Joseph	*pray for us*
Saint Peter and Saint Paul	*pray for us*
Saint Andrew	*pray for us*
Saint John	*pray for us*
Saint Mary Magdalene	*pray for us*
Saint Stephen	*pray for us*
Saint Ignatius of Antioch	*pray for us*
Saint Lawrence	*pray for us*
Saint Perpetua and Saint Felicity	*pray for us*
Saint Agnes	*pray for us*
Saint Gregory	*pray for us*
Saint Augustine	*pray for us*
Saint Athanasius	*pray for us*
Saint Basil	*pray for us*
Saint Martin	*pray for us*
Saint Benedict	*pray for us*
Saint Francis and Saint Dominic	*pray for us*
Saint Francis Xavier	*pray for us*
Saint John Vianney	*pray for us*
Saint Catherine of Siena	*pray for us*
Saint Teresa of Jesus	*pray for us*
(Other names of saints may be added.)	*(pray for us)*

All holy men and women, Saints of God	*pray for us*

Lord, be merciful	*Lord, deliver us, we pray*
From all evil	*Lord, deliver us, we pray*
From every sin	*Lord, deliver us, we pray*
From everlasting death	*Lord, deliver us, we pray*
By your Incarnation	*Lord, deliver us, we pray*
By your Death and Resurrection	*Lord, deliver us, we pray*
By the outpouring of the Holy Spirit	*Lord, deliver us, we pray*

Be merciful to us sinners	*Lord, we ask you, hear our prayer*
Guide and protect your holy Church	*Lord, we ask you, hear our prayer*
Keep the pope and all the clergy in faithful service to your Church	*Lord, we ask you, hear our prayer*
Bring all peoples together in trust and peace	*Lord, we ask you, hear our prayer*
Strengthen us in your service	*Lord, we ask you, hear our prayer*
Jesus, Son of the living God	*Lord, we ask you, hear our prayer*
Christ, hear us	*Christ, hear us*
Christ, graciously hear us	*Christ, graciously hear us*

Let us pray.

God of our ancestors who set their hearts on you,
of those who fell asleep in peace,
and of those who won the martyrs' violent crown:
we are surrounded by these witnesses
as by clouds of fragrant incense.
In this age we would be counted
in the communion of all the saints;
keep us always in their good and blessed company.
In their midst we make every prayer
through Christ who is our Lord for ever and ever.
℟. *Amen.*

30

Magnificat

Canticle of Mary

✠ My soul proclaims the greatness of the Lord,
my spirit rejoices in God my Savior;
for he has looked with favor on his lowly servant.

From this day all generations will call me blessed:
the Almighty has done great things for me,
and holy is his Name.

He has mercy on those who fear him
in every generation.

He has shown the strength of his arm,
he has scattered the proud in their conceit.

He has cast down the mighty from their thrones,
and has lifted up the lowly.

He has filled the hungry with good things,
and the rich he has sent away empty.

He has come to the help of his servant Israel
for he has remembered his promise of mercy,
the promise he made to our fathers,
to Abraham and his children for ever.

[Glory to the Father, and to the Son, and to the Holy Spirit:
as it was in the beginning, is now, and will be for ever.
    Amen.]

A *partial indulgence* is granted the Christian faithful
who devoutly recite the canticle called the *Magnificat*.

31

Maria, Mater gratiae

A Child's Prayer to Mary

Mary, mother whom we bless,
full of grace and tenderness,
defend me from the devil's power
and greet me in my dying hour.

A partial indulgence.

32

Memorare, o piissime Virgo Maria

The Memorare

Remember, most loving Virgin Mary,
never was it heard
that anyone who turned to you for help
was left unaided.

Inspired by this confidence,
though burdened by my sins,
I run to your protection
for you are my mother.

Mother of the Word of God,
do not despise my words of pleading
but be merciful and hear my prayer.
Amen.

A partial indulgence.

33

Miserere

Psalm 51

A *partial indulgence* is granted the Christian faithful who recite the Miserere, psalm 51, in a spirit of penitence.

Have mercy on me, God, in your goodness;
in your abundant compassion blot out my offense.
Wash away all my guilt;
from my sin cleanse me.

For I know my offense;
my sin is always before me.
Against you alone have I sinned;
I have done such evil in your sight
That you are just in your sentence,
blameless when you condemn.

True, I was born guilty,
a sinner, even as my mother conceived me.
Still, you insist on sincerity of heart;
in my inmost being teach me wisdom.

Cleanse me with hyssop, that I may be pure;
wash me, make me whiter than snow.
Let me hear sounds of joy and gladness;
let the bones you have crushed rejoice.

Turn away your face from my sins;
blot out all my guilt.
A clean heart create for me, God;
renew in me a steadfast spirit.

Do not drive me from your presence,
nor take from me your holy spirit.
Restore my joy in your salvation;
sustain in me a willing spirit.

I will teach the wicked your ways,
that sinners may return to you.

Rescue me from death, God, my saving God,
that my tongue may praise your healing power.

Lord, open my lips;
my mouth will proclaim your praise.
For you do not desire sacrifice;
a burnt offering you would not accept.
My sacrifice, God, is a broken spirit;
God, do not spurn a broken, humbled heart.

Make Zion prosper in your good pleasure;
rebuild the walls of Jerusalem.
Then you will be pleased with proper sacrifice,
burnt offerings and holocausts;
then bullocks will be offered on your altar.

[Glory to the Father, and to the Son, and to the Holy Spirit:
as it was in the beginning, is now, and will be for ever.
    Amen.]

34

Novendiales preces

Novena Prayers

A *partial indulgence* is granted the Christian faithful
who devoutly take part in a publicly celebrated novena before the solemnity of Christmas, Pentecost, or the Immaculate Conception of the Blessed Virgin Mary.

35

Obiectorum pietatis usus

Use of Devotional Objects

The Christian faithful obtain a *partial indulgence* when they make devout use of a devotional object (such as a crucifix or cross, a rosary, a scapular, or a medal) which has been rightly blessed by any priest or deacon.[3]

If the devotional object has been blessed by the Pope or by any bishop, the Christian faithful can obtain a *plenary indulgence* while making devout use of it on the solemnity of the holy apostles, Peter and Paul, provided they add to its use a profession of faith made in any legitimate formula.

This grant is taken from the apostolic constitution *Indulgentiarum doctrina*, norm 16. See also above, norm 19, p. 21.

36

Officia parva

Little Offices

The following Little Offices are endowed with a *partial indulgence:* the Little Office of the Passion of Our Lord Jesus Christ; the Little Office of the Sacred Heart of Jesus; the Little Office of the Blessed Virgin Mary; the Little Office of the Immaculate Conception; and the Little Office of Saint Joseph.

---

[3] To bless devotional objects rightly the priest or deacon should observe the liturgical formularies prescribed in the *Book of Blessings* from the Roman Ritual. In this matter, however, it is worth noting that a sign of the cross is sufficient for the blessing, although it is recommended that the words, "In the name of the Father, and of the Son, and of the Holy Spirit," be added. Cf. Roman Ritual, *De Benedictionibus*, numbers 1165 and 1182 (Latin edition) [U.S. ed.: *Book of Blessings*, nos. 1466 and 1487].

37

Oratio ad sacerdotales vel religiosas
vocationes impetrandas

Prayer for Priestly and Religious Vocations

A *partial indulgence* is granted the Christian faithful
who recite a prayer approved for this purpose by ecclesiastical authority. (The following prayer has received such approval.)

Lord,
in your love for the Church,
you provide bishops, priests and deacons
as shepherds for your people,
and you call men and women to leave all things
to serve you joyfully in religious life.

May those whom you have raised up
as servants of the Gospel and ministers for your altars
show forth dedication and compassion.

May those whom you have chosen to serve you as religious
provide by their way of life
a convincing sign of your kingdom
for the Church and the whole world.

We ask this through Christ our Lord.
℟. *Amen.*

38

Oratio mentalis

Mental Prayer

A *partial indulgence* is granted the Christian faithful
who devoutly spent time in mental prayer.

39

Oremus pro Pontifice

Prayer for the Pope

Let us pray for N., our pope.
May the Lord protect him
and grant him length of days.
Amen.

May the Lord be his shield
and deliver him from all harm.
Amen

May the Lord give him happiness and peace
all the days of his life.
Amen.

A partial indulgence.

40

O sacrum convivium

How Holy This Feast

How holy this feast
in which Christ is our food:
his passion is recalled,
grace fills our hearts,
and we receive a pledge of the glory to come.

℣. You gave them bread from heaven to be their food.
℟. *And this bread contained all goodness.*

Let us pray.

Lord Jesus Christ,
you gave us the eucharist
as the memorial of your suffering and death.
May our worship of this sacrament of your body and blood
help us to experience the salvation you won for us
and the peace of the kingdom

where you live with the Father and the Holy Spirit,
one God, for ever and ever.
Ꝝ. *Amen.*

> (Roman Ritual, *Holy Communion and Worship of the Eucharist outside Mass,* nos. 65, 200.)

A partial indulgence.

41

Praedicationis sacrae participatio

Listening to Preaching

A *partial indulgence* is granted the Christian faithful who attentively and devoutly assist at the preaching of the Word of God.

A *plenary indulgence* is granted the Christian faithful who on the occasion of a mission have heard some of the sermons and are present for its solemn conclusion.

42

Prima Communio

First Communion

A *plenary indulgence* is granted the Christian faithful when they receive their first communion and also when they devoutly assist at a first communion ceremony.

43

Prima Missa neosacerdotum

First Mass of Newly Ordained Priests

A *plenary indulgence* is granted a priest celebrating his first Mass with a congregation on a scheduled day. The same indulgence is also granted the faithful who devoutly participate in that Mass.

44

Pro christianorum unitate oratio

Prayer for the Unity of Christians

Almighty and eternal God,
you gather the scattered sheep
and watch over those you have gathered.

Look kindly on all who follow Jesus, your Son.

You have marked them with the seal of one baptism;
now make them one in the fullness of faith
and unite them in the bond of love.

We ask this through Christ our Lord.
℟. *Amen.*

   A partial indulgence.

45

Recollectio menstrua

Monthly Period of Recollection

A *partial indulgence* is granted the Christian faithful
who participate in a monthly period of recollection.

46

Requiem aeternam

Prayer for the Dead

Eternal rest grant unto them, O Lord,
and let perpetual light shine upon them.
May they rest in peace. Amen.

   (Cf. Roman Ritual, *The Order of Christian Funerals.*)

   A *partial indulgence*, applicable only to the souls in purgatory.

47

Retribuere dignare, Domine

Prayer for Benefactors

Reward those who have been good to us
for the sake of your name, O Lord,
and give them eternal life.
Amen.

A partial indulgence.

48

Rosarii marialis recitatio

Recitation of the Marian Rosary

A *plenary indulgence* is granted when the rosary is recited in a church or oratory or when it is recited in a family,
a religious community, or a pious association. A *partial
indulgence* is granted for its recitation in all other circumstances.

(The rosary is a prayer formula divided into fifteen decades of Hail Mary's with the *Lord's Prayer* separating each
of these decades. During each of these decades we recall in
devout meditation the mysteries of our redemption.)

It has become customary to call but five such decades
the "rosary" also. Concerning this customary usage then,
the following norms are given as regards a plenary indulgence.

1. The recitation of a third of the rosary is sufficient for
obtaining the *plenary indulgence,* but these five decades
must be recited without interruption.

2. Devout meditation on the mysteries is to be added to
the vocal prayer.

3. In its public recitation the mysteries must be announced in accord with approved local custom, but in its private recitation it is sufficient for the Christian faithful simply to join meditation on the mysteries to the vocal prayer.

4. In the Eastern Churches where recitation of the Marian rosary as a devotional practice is not found, the patriarchs can establish other prayers in honor of the blessed Virgin Mary which will have the same indulgences as those attached to the rosary, (e.g., in the Byzantine churches, the Akathist hymn, or the office *Paraclisis.)*

49

Sacerdotalis Ordinationis celebrationes iubilares

Jubilee Celebrations of Priestly Ordination

A *plenary indulgence* is granted to a priest who on his 25th, 50th, and 60th anniversary of priestly ordination renews before God the promise made by him to faithfully fulfill the duties of his vocation.

And when the Christian faithful participate in the jubilee Mass celebrated by the priest, they also can obtain a *plenary indulgence.*

50

Sacrae Scripturae lectio

Reading the Sacred Scriptures

A *partial indulgence* is granted the Christian faithful who read sacred scripture with the veneration due God's word and as a form of spiritual reading. The indulgence will be a *plenary* one when such reading is done for at least one-half hour.

---

* See p. 123 for the 1991 decree of the Sacred Apostolic Penitentiary concerning the Akathist hymn.

51

Salve, Regina

Hail, Holy Queen

Hail, holy Queen, Mother of mercy,
hail, our life, our sweetness, and our hope.
To you we cry, the children of Eve;
to you we send up our sighs,
mourning and weeping in this land of exile.
Turn, then, most gracious advocate,
your eyes of mercy toward us;
lead us home at last
and show us the blessed fruit of your womb, Jesus:
O clement, O loving, O sweet Virgin Mary.

(The Liturgy of the Hours, Night Prayer.)

A partial indulgence.

52

Sancta Maria, succurre miseris

Mary, Help of Those in Need

Holy Mary,
help those in need,
give strength to the weak,
comfort the sorrowful,
pray for God's people,
assist the clergy,
intercede for religious.

May all who seek your help
experience your unfailing protection.
Amen.

A partial indulgence.

53

Sancti Apostoli Petre et Paule

Invocation to Saints Peter and Paul

Saints Peter and Paul, pray for us.
Lord, come to the aid of your people,
who rely on the help of your holy apostles;
protect us and be our defense for ever.
We ask this through Christ our Lord.
Amen.

A partial indulgence

54

Sanctorum cultus

Cult of the Saints

A *partial indulgence* is granted the Christian faithful who on the day of the liturgical feast of any saint recite in that saint's honor the prayer taken from the missal or another prayer approved by legitimate authority.

55

Signum crucis

Sign of the Cross

A *partial indulgence* is granted the Christian faithful who devoutly sign themselves with the cross while saying the customary formula: "In the name of the Father, and of the Son, and of the Holy Spirit. Amen."

56

Stationalium ecclesiarum visitatio

Visiting the Stational Churches

A *partial indulgence* is granted the Christian faithful who devoutly visit a stational church on its stational day. The indulgence will be a plenary one if they also take part in the morning or evening services conducted in that church. (Cf. the *Ceremonial for Bishops*, numbers 260-261.)

57

Sub tuum praesidium

Ancient Prayer to the Virgin

We turn to you for protection,
holy Mother of God.
Listen to our prayers
and help us in our needs.
Save us from every danger,
glorious and blessed Virgin.

(The Liturgy of the Hours, Night Prayer.)

A partial indulgence.

58

Synodus dioecesana

Diocesan Synod

A *plenary indulgence* is granted for one time only to the Christian faithful who, during the time of a diocesan synod, devoutly visit the church in which the synod is held and there recite the Lord's Prayer and the Creed.

59

Tantum ergo

Secret Past Imagination

Secret past imagination, dazzling and compelling awe;
Sacrament and celebration richer than the ancient law:
Faith can see by revelation more than senses ever saw.

Praise the Lord with exultation for the marvels he has done:
Blessing, power, and adoration to the Father and the Son
For creation and salvation; and the Spirit, Three in One.
  Amen.

℣. You gave them bread from heaven to be their food.
℟. *And this bread contained all goodness.*

Let us pray.

Lord Jesus Christ,
you gave us the eucharist
as the memorial of your suffering and death.
May our worship of this sacrament of your body and
  blood
help us to experience the salvation you won for us
and the peace of the kingdom
where you live with the Father and the Holy Spirit,
one God, for ever and ever.

℟. *Amen.*

> (Roman Ritual, *Holy Communion and Worship of the Eucharist
> outside Mass*, nos. 97 and 98.)

A *partial indulgence* is granted the Christian faithful who
devoutly recite the above verses. The indulgence will be a
plenary one on Holy Thursday after the Mass of the Lord's
Supper and on the solemnity of the Body and Blood of
Christ during its liturgical rites.

60

Te Deum

You are God: We Praise You

You are God: we praise you;
You are the Lord: we acclaim you;
You are the eternal Father:
All creation worships you.

To you all angels, all the powers of heaven,
Cherubim and Seraphim, sing in endless praise:
> Holy, holy, holy Lord, God of power and might,
> heaven and earth are full of your glory.

The glorious company of apostles praise you.
The noble fellowship of prophets praise you.
The white-robed army of martyrs praise you.

Throughout the world the holy Church acclaims you:
> Father, of majesty unbounded,
> your true and only Son, worthy of all worship,
> and the Holy Spirit, advocate and guide.

You, Christ, are the king of glory,
the eternal Son of the Father.

When you became man to set us free
you did not spurn the Virgin's womb.

You overcame the sting of death,
and opened the kingdom of heaven to all believers.

You are seated at God's right hand in glory.
We believe that you will come, and be our judge.

Come then, Lord, and help your people,
bought with the price of your own blood,
and bring us with your saints
to glory everlasting.

℣. Save your people, Lord, and bless your inheritance.
℟. *Govern and uphold them now and always.*

℣. Day by day we bless you.
℟. *We praise your name for ever.*

℣. Keep us today, Lord, from all sin.
℟. *Have mercy on us, Lord, have mercy.*

℣. Lord, show us your love and mercy;
℟. *for we put our trust in you.*

℣. In you, Lord, is our hope:
℟. *and we shall never hope in vain.*

A *partial indulgence* is granted the Christian faithful who recite the hymn, *Te Deum*, as an act of thanksgiving. The indulgence will be a *plenary* one if this hymn is publicly recited on the last day of the year.

61

Veni, Creator

Come, Creator Spirit

O Holy Spirit, by whose breath
Life rises vibrant out of death;
Come to create, renew, inspire;
Come, kindle in our hearts your fire.

You are the seeker's sure resource,
Of burning love the living source,
Protector in the midst of strife,
The giver and the Lord of life.

In you God's energy is shown,
To us your varied gifts made known.
Teach us to speak, teach us to hear;
Yours is the tongue and yours the ear.

Flood our dull senses with your light;
In mutual love our hearts unite.
Your power the whole creation fills;
Confirm our weak, uncertain wills.

From inner strife grant us release;
Turn nations to the ways of peace.
To fuller life your people bring
That as one body we may sing:

Praise to the Father, Christ, his Word,
And to the Spirit: God the Lord,
To whom all honor, glory be
Both now and for eternity. Amen.

Att. Rabanus Maurus (776-856); tr. John Webster Grant (b. 1919), alt. *(Hymnbook 1982, no. 502).*

A *partial indulgence* is granted the Christian faithful who devoutly recite the hymn, *Veni, Creator.* The indulgence will be a *plenary* one when this hymn is recited publicly on the first day of January and on the solemnity of Pentecost.

62

Veni, Sancte Spiritus

Come, Holy Spirit

℣. Come, Holy Spirit, fill the hearts of your faithful.
℟. *And kindle in them the fire of your love.*

℣. Send forth your Spirit and they shall be created.
℟. *And you will renew the face of the earth.*

Let us pray.

Lord,
by the light of the Holy Spirit
you have taught the hearts of your faithful.
In the same Spirit
help us to relish what is right
and always rejoice in your consolation.

We ask this through Christ our Lord.
℟. *Amen.*

A partial indulgence.

63

Viae Crucis exercitium

Stations of the Cross

A *plenary indulgence* is granted the Christian faithful who devoutly make the Stations of the Cross. This devout exercise of the Stations of the Cross helps renew our remembrance of the sufferings which our divine redeemer underwent on his journey from Pilate's praetorium, where he was condemned to death, to Mount Calvary, where for our salvation he died on the cross.

The norms for obtaining this plenary indulgence are the following:

1. This devout excercise must be performed before stations of the cross which have been lawfully erected.

2. Fourteen crosses are required in order to erect the Stations of the Cross. As an aid to devotion these crosses are customarily attached to fourteen tableaux or images representing the Jerusalem stations.

3. In accord with the more common custom, this devout exercise consists of fourteen pious readings to which are joined some vocal prayers. But in order to perform this devout exercise it is required only that one devoutly meditate upon the passion and death of the Lord. It is not required that one meditate upon each of the individual mysteries of the stations.

4. Movement from one station to the next is required. If this devout exercise is carried out publicly and such movement by all present cannot be done without some disorder, it is sufficient that the person who is leading the exercise move from station to station while the others remain in their places.

5. Persons who are legitimately prevented from fulfilling the above requirements can obtain this indulgence if

they at least spend some time, e.g., fifteen minutes, in devout reading and meditation upon the passion and death of our Lord Jesus Christ.

6. Equivalent to this devout exercise of the Stations of the Cross—even with regard to obtaining the indulgence—are those other devout exercises which have been approved by competent authority and which call to mind the remembrance of the Lord's passion and death in a manner similar to the Stations of the Cross.

7. In order to obtain this indulgence, the patriarchs can establish some other devout exercise in memory of the passion and death of our Lord Jesus Christ for those Eastern Christian faithful whose usages do not include this exercise of the Stations.

64

Visita, quaesumus, Domine

A Night Prayer

Visit this house,
we beg you, Lord,
and banish from it
the deadly power of the evil one.
May your holy angels dwell here
to keep us in peace,
and may your blessing be always upon us.

We ask this through Christ our Lord.
Amen.

> (The Liturgy of the Hours, Night Prayer after Sunday Evening Prayer.)

> *A partial indulgence.*

65

Visitatio ecclesiae paroecialis

Visiting a Parish Church

A *plenary indulgence* is granted the Christian faithful who devoutly make a visit to a parish church:

1) on its titular feast day;

2) on August 2, the day on which the *Portiuncula* indulgence occurs.

These same indulgences can be obtained either on the days mentioned above or on other days determined by the ordinary so that the faithful can take better advantage of them.

The same indulgences are also attached to the cathedral church and, if there be one, to the co-cathedral church, even if neither of these is a parish church. They are also attached to a quasi-parish church.[4]

These indulgences are already contained in the apostolic constitution, Indulgentiarum doctrina, *norm 15. They are included here in light of the Sacred Penitentiary's deliberations since the constitution was issued.*

According to norm 16 of the apostolic constitution, this visit is to include the "recitation of the Lord's Prayer and the Creed (Pater *and* Credo).*"*[5]

66

Visitatio ecclesiae vel altaris die dedicationis

Visiting a Church or an Altar on the Day of its Dedication

A *plenary indulgence* is granted the Christian faithful who devoutly visit a church or altar on the same day it is dedicated and recite there the Lord's Prayer and the Creed.

---

[4] Cf. *Code of Canon Law*, canon 516, paragraph 1.

[5] Confer also above, norm 25, page 23.

67

Visitatio ecclesiae vel oratorii in
Commemoratione omnium fidelium defunctorum

Visiting a Church or an Oratory on All Souls Day

A *plenary indulgence* which is applicable only to the souls in purgatory is granted the Christian faithful who devoutly visit a church or an oratory on All Souls Day.

This indulgence can be obtained either on the day mentioned above or, with the consent of the ordinary, on the preceding or following Sunday or on the solemnity of All Saints.

This indulgence is already contained in the apostolic constitution, Indulgentiarum doctrina, *norm 15. It is included here in light of the Sacred Penitentiary's deliberations since the constitution was issued.*

According to norm 16 of the apostolic constitution, this visit is to include the "recitation of the Lord's Prayer and the Creed (Pater *and* Credo).*"*[6]

68

Visitatio ecclesiae vel oratorii Religiosorum
die eorum Fundatori sacro

Visiting a Church or an Oratory of Religious on a Day Dedicated to their Founder

A *plenary indulgence* is granted the Christian faithful who devoutly visit a church or an oratory of Religious on a day dedicated to their founder and there recite the Pater and the Credo.

---

[6] Confer also above, norm 22, page 22.

69

Visitatio pastoralis

Pastoral Visitation

A *partial indulgence* is granted the Christian faithful who devoutly visit a church or an oratory during the time when a pastoral visitation is being conducted there. The indulgence is a *plenary* one, to be obtained but once, if during the time of the pastoral visitation they participate in a religious service over which the visitor presides.

70

Votorum baptismalium renovatio

Renewal of Baptismal Promises

A *partial indulgence* is granted the Christian faithful who renew their baptismal promises through any customary formula. When they do this during the celebration of the Easter Vigil or on the anniversary of their own baptism, they obtain a *plenary* indulgence.

℣. Do you renounce sin,
    so as to live in the freedom of the children of God?
℟. *I do.*

℣. Do you renounce the lure of evil,
    so that sin may have no mastery over you?
℟. *I do.*

℣. Do you renounce Satan,
    the author and prince of sin?
℟. *I do.*

℣. Do you believe in God,
    the Father almighty,
    Creator of heaven and earth?
℟. *I do.*

℣. Do you believe in Jesus Christ, his only Son, our Lord,
who was born of the Virgin Mary,
suffered death and was buried,
rose again from the dead
and is seated at the right hand of the Father?
℟. *I do.*

℣. Do you believe in the Holy Spirit,
the holy Catholic Church,
the communion of saints,
the forgiveness of sins,
the resurrection of the body,
and life everlasting?
℟. *I do.*

℣. This is our faith. This is the faith of the Church.
We are proud to profess it in Christ Jesus our Lord.
℟. *Amen.*

APPENDIX

PIOUS INVOCATIONS

The following points are to be noted in regard to any pious invocation:

1. In its relationship to an indulgence an invocation is not to be considered as something distinct and complete in and of itself. It is to be considered as a complementary adjunct to some work. By using such an invocation the Christian faithful raise up their minds in trust to God while carrying out their duties of life and putting up with the difficulties of life. Thus a pious invocation complements that raising up of one's mind to God. Both the raising up of the mind and the pious invocation are like a precious stone which is inserted into one's everyday activities and embellishes them, or they are like salt which suitably seasons those activities.

2. That invocation is to be preferred which is more in touch with present day realities and attitudes. Such invocations can arise spontaneously in one's mind, or they can be chosen from among those which have gained acceptance through their long-standing use by the Christian faithful. A short listing of some of these latter are found below.

3. An invocation can be very short, expressed in but one or a few words or conceived only mentally.

Some examples may be of help: "My God"; "Father"; "Jesus"; "Praised be Jesus Christ" (or some other customary Christian greeting); "I believe in you, Lord"; "I adore you"; "I hope in you"; "I love you"; "All for you"; "I give you thanks" (or, "Thank God"); "Blessed be God" (or "Let us bless the Lord"); "Your kingdom come"; "Your will be done"; "May it be as God pleases"; "Help me, God"; "Give me strength"; "Hear me" (or, "Listen to my prayer"); "Save me"; "Have pity on me"; "Forgive me, Lord"; "Do not permit me to be separated from you"; "Do not forsake me"; "Hail, Mary"; "Glory to God in the highest"; "Lord, you are great."

SOME EXAMPLES OF INVOCATIONS
IN CURRENT USAGE

1. We adore you, O Christ, and we bless you:
    because by your holy cross you have redeemed the
    world.

2. Blessed be the Holy Trinity.

3. Christ is victor, Christ is ruler, Christ is Lord of all.

4. Heart of Jesus, burning with love for us,
    inflame our hearts with love for you.

5. Heart of Jesus, I trust in you.

6. Heart of Jesus, all for love of you.

7. Sacred Heart of Jesus, have mercy on us.

8. My God and my all.

9. Lord, be merciful to me, a sinner.   (Lk 18:13)

10. Let me praise you, Virgin most holy:
    give me strength against your enemies.

11. Teach me to do your will, for you are my God.
                                                (Ps 143:10)

12. Lord, increase our faith.   (Lk 17:5)

13. Lord, make our minds one in truth
    and our hearts one in love.

14. Lord, save us or we perish   (Mt 8:25)

15. My Lord and my God.   (Jn 20:28)

16. Loving heart of Mary, be my refuge.

17. Glory to the Father, and to the Son, and to the Holy Spirit:
    [as it was in the beginning, is now, and will be for ever. Amen.]

18. Jesus, Mary, and Joseph.

19. Jesus, Mary, and Joseph, I give you my heart and my soul.
    Jesus, Mary, and Joseph, assist me in the hour of my death.
    Jesus, Mary, and Joseph, may I die and rest in peace with you.

20. Jesus, gentle and humble of heart, make my heart like yours.

21. May the blessed sacrament be praised and adored for ever.

22. Stay with us, Lord.

23. Mother of sorrows, pray for us.

24. My Mother, my hope.

25. Lord, send laborers into your harvest.

26. May the Virgin Mary bless us with her child.

27. Hail, O Cross, our only hope.

28. All holy men and women, pray for us.

29. Pray for us, holy Mother of God,
    that we may become worthy of the promises of Christ.

30. Father, into your hands I commend my spirit.

31. Lord Jesus, in your mercy grant them eternal rest.

32. Queen conceived without original sin, pray for us.

33. Holy Mother of God, ever Virgin Mary, intercede for us.

34. Holy Mary, Mother of God, pray for me.

35. You are the Christ, the Son of the living God.

DOCUMENTATION

Paul VI, Apostolic constitution *Indulgentiarum doctrina,* on indulgences, 1 January 1967: AAS 59 (1967) 5-24.*

I

1. The teaching and practice regarding indulgences prevailing for centuries in the Catholic Church rest on divine revelation as their firm foundation.[1] This revelation, handed on by the apostles, "develops in the Church under the influence of the Holy Spirit" as "... with the passage of the centuries the Church advances toward the fullness of divine truth until in it God's words are wholly accomplished."[2]

In the interest of a right understanding of the teaching on indulgences and its sound application it is our responsibility to call attention to certain truths. The whole Church, enlightened by God's word, has always believed these truths and, both through pastoral practice and through doctrinal statements, the bishops, successors of the apostles, and above all the popes, successors of St. Peter, have taught them down through the years and do so still.

2. As divine revelations teaches, punishment inflicted by God's holiness and justice is the consequence of sin. Such punishment is to be borne in this world through the

---

* This translation is a slight revision of the one found in *Documents on the Liturgy, 1963-1978: Conciliar, Papal, and Curial Texts* © 1982, ICEL. The abbreviations are those used therein (DOL) and listed on pp. 1437-1441.

[1] See Council of Trent, sess. 25, *Decr. de indulgentiis:* "The power of granting indulgences has been given to the Church by Christ and the Church has used this divinely bestowed power even from its earliest days ...": Denz-Schön 1835. See Mt 28:18.

[2] DV no. 8 [DOL 14, no. 221]. See also Vatican Council I, Dogmatic Const. De fide catholica *Dei Filius,* cap. 4, De fide et ratione: Denz-Schön 3020.

99

pain, miseries, and hardships of the present life, above all through death,[3] or in the world to come through the fire and torments of hell or the purifying pains of purgatory.[4] The faithful of Christ have thus always had the conviction that the path of evil has many stumbling blocks and that it is a rough and thorny path, lethal to those who follow it.[5]

A just and merciful judgment of God enjoins such punishments: they are meant to purge the soul, to protect the inviolability of the moral order, and to restore the divine glory to its full majesty. With respect to the last point, every sin involves the upsetting of the general order that in his inexpressible wisdom and boundless charity God has laid out;

---

[3] See Gn 3:16-19: "To the woman he said: 'I will greatly multiply your pain in childbearing: in pain you shall bring forth children. Yet your desire shall be for your husband and he shall rule you.' To the man he said: 'Because you have listened to your wife and have eaten from the tree of which I commanded that you were not to eat of it, cursed is the ground because of you. In toil you shall eat of it all the days of your life. It shall bring forth to you thorns and thistles. . . . In the sweat of your face you shall eat bread till you return to the ground, for out of it you were taken. You are dust, and to dust you shall return.' "

See also Lk 19:41-44; Rom 2:9; 1 Cor 11:30.

See Augustine, *Enarr. in Ps. 58* 1, 13: "Every iniquity, great or small, must be punished, whether by the sinner's repentance or by God's vengeance": CCL 39, 739; PL 36, 701.

See ST 1a2ae, 87.1: "Since sin is an act that lacks due order, it is clear that whoever sins is in conflict with some kind of order. Therefore the sinner is repressed by that order. Such repression is what punishment is."

[4] See Mt 25:41-42: "Depart from me, you accursed, into the everlasting fire prepared for the devil and his angels. For I was hungry and you did not feed me." See also Mk 9:42-43; Jn 5:28-29; Rom 2:9; Gal 6:6-8.

See Council of Lyons II, sess. 4, *Professio fidei Michaelis Palaeologi imperatoris:* Denz-Schön 856-858.

See Council of Florence, *Decr. pro Graecis:* Denz-Schön 1304-06.

See Augustine, *Enchiridion* 66, 17: "Many things seem in this life to be forgiven and to go unavenged by punishment, but their punishment is being kept for the hereafter. For it is not in vain that the day on which the judge of the living and the dead is to come bears the name 'judgment day.' On the other hand, some things are avenged in this life, but if they are remitted they will cause no suffering in the world to come. Thus with regard to certain temporal punishments exacted of sinners in this life, St. Paul advises those whose sins are pardoned how to avoid such punishments being stored up until the end: 'If we would judge ourselves we should not be judged. But when we are judged, we are chastened by the Lord that we should not be chastened by the world' (1 Cor 11:31-32)": Scheel, ed. (Tübingen, 1930) 42; 4L 40, 263.

[5] See *Hermes Pastor*, Mand. 6, 1, 3: Funk PA 1, 487.

sin also involves the destruction of supreme values, pertaining both to the individual sinner and the entire human community. To the mind of Christians of every era it has been absolutely clear that sin is a transgression of the divine law, but over and above that, even if not directly and flagrantly, a contempt or neglect toward the personal friendship between God and each person;[6] that it is a real and never adequately measured offense against God, an ungrateful rejection of God's love offered to us in Christ. For Christ has called us his friends, not his servants.[7]

3. For the complete pardon of sins and for their reparation, as it is called, it is thus necessary that a genuine conversion of spirit restore friendship with God and make expiation for the affront to his wisdom and goodness. But more than that, it is necessary that all the values, personal, social, and those forming part of the general order that sin has undermined or destroyed, be fully reestablished, either through voluntary, punitive reparation or through the bearing of those punishments decreed by God's just and absolutely holy wisdom. The sanctity and splendor of God's glory will thus be made to shine forth throughout the world. For the fact and the severity of punishment manifest the folly and wickedness of sin and its evil consequences.

---

[6] See Is 1:2-3: "I have reared and brought up sons, but they have rebelled against me. The ox knew its owner and the ass its master's crib; but Israel does not know, my people do not understand." See also Dt 8:11 and 32:15ff.; Ps 105 [106]:21 and 118 [119] passim; Wis 7:14; Is 17:10 and 44:21; Jer 33:8; Ex 20:27.

See DV no. 2: "Thus by this revelation the unseen God (see Col 1:15; 1 Tm 1:17) speaks to us as his friends from the abundance of his love (see Ex 33:11; Jn 15:14-15) and communicates with us (see Bar 3:38) in order to invite us and welcome us into a communion with him": AAS 58 (1966) 818; ConstDecrDecl 424; see also DV no. 21 [Dol 14, no. 224].

[7] See Jn 15:14-15. See also GS no. 22; AAS 58 (1966) 1042; ConstDecrDecl 709-710; AG no. 13: AAS 58 (1966) 962; ConstDecrDecl 568.

The teaching on purgatory clearly shows that punishments to be borne or the remnants of sin to be purged can remain and often do remain even after the sin has been pardoned.[8] For in purgatory the souls of the dead who "have died truly repentant in God's love, before they have atoned for their sins and omissions by the worthy fruits of repentance"[9] are cleansed after death by the pains of purgatory. The prayers of the liturgy point to the same fact: the Christian community from earliest times in the celebration of the eucharist has used these prayers to plead "that we who are justly afflicted for our sins may mercifully be delivered for the glory of your name."[10]

All of us, pilgrims in this world, commit at least light and, as they are called, daily sins;[11] we are all therefore in

---

[8] See Nm 20:12: "And the Lord said to Moses and Aaron: 'Because you did not believe in me, to sanctify me in the eyes of the people of Israel, therefore you should not bring this assembly into the land that I have given them.' "

See Nm 27:13-14: "And when you have seen it, you also shall be gathered to your people, as your brother Aaron was gathered, because you rebelled against my word in the wilderness of Zith, to sanctify me in the waters before their eyes."

See 2 Sm 12:13-14: "And David said to Nathan: 'I have sinned against the Lord.' And Nathan said to David: 'The Lord also has put away your sin; you shall not die. Nevertheless, because by this deed you have utterly scorned the Lord, the child that is born to you shall die.' "

See Innocent IV, *Instructio pro Graecis:* Denz-Schön 838.

See Council of Trent, sess. 6, can. 30: "Let anyone be anathema who would say that after having the grace of justification a sinner receives pardon for sin and release from the debt of eternal punishment in such a way that no debt of temporal punishment remains, to be acquitted in this life or in the world to come in purgatory, before the sinner's admittance to the kingdom of heaven is possible": Denz-Schön 1580; see also Denz-Schön 1689, 1963.

See Augustine, *In Io. Ev. tract.* 124,5: "We are obliged to suffer in this life even after our sins have been pardoned, although original sin was the reason why we have fallen into this plight. For punishment lasts longer than sin so that sin is not regarded lightly, as would be the case were the punishment ended without the end of the sin. Thus even when sin no longer holds us bound to eternal damnation, temporal punishment still is binding on us, either as a sign of the misery we have earned, as a corrective against a sinful life, or as an exercise in the patience we need": CCL 36, 683-684; PL 35 1972-73.

[9] Council of Lyons II, sess. 4: Denz-Schön 856.

[10] See MR, Septuagesima Sunday, collect: "We ask you, O Lord, hear the prayers of your people: that we who are justly afflicted for our sins may mercifully be delivered for the glory of your name."

See MR, Monday of the First Week of Lent, prayer over the people: "Loosen, O Lord, the bonds of our sins and graciously prevent whatever we have deserved because of them."

See MR, Third Sunday of Lent, prayer after communion: "O Lord, graciously deliver from all guilt and peril those whom you favor with a share in so great a mystery."

need of God's mercy for deliverance from sin's penal consequences.

II

4. The hidden and gracious mystery of God's design unites us all through a supernatural bond: on this basis one person's sin harms the rest even as one person's goodness enriches them.[12] As a result, the faithful help one another to attain this supernatural destiny. The sign of their communion is expressed in Adam: his sin passes to us all on the basis of procreation. But the far greater and more complete source, foundation, and model of this supernatural bond is Christ: communion with him is the vocation God has given to us all.[13]

---

[11] See Jas 3:2: "We all fail in many things."

See 1 Jn 1:8: "If we say we have no sin, we deceive ourselves and the truth is not in us." On this text the Council of Carthage comments: "The Council also has decided with regard to the words of St. John the Apostle" [text quoted] "to anathematize anyone of the opinion that they are to be taken to mean that we should say we have sinned as a sign of humility, not as a statement of truth": Denz-Schön 228.

See Council of Trent, sess. 6, *Decr. de iustificatione* cap. 2: Denz-Schön 1537.

See LG no. 40: "Because we all offend in many matters (see Jas 3:2), we are continually in need of God's mercy and must pray daily 'Forgive us our sins' (Mt 6:12).": AAS 57 (1965) 45; ConstDecrDecl 166.

[12] See Augustine, *De bapt. contra Donat.* 1, 28: PL 43, 124.

[13] See Jn 15:15: "I am the vine, you are the branches: all who abide in me and I in them bear much fruit."

See 1 Cor 12:27: "Now you are the Body of Christ and every one of you a member of it." See also 1 Cor 1:9-10 and 17; Eph 1:20-23; 4:4.

See LG no. 7 [DOL 4, no. 139].

See Pius XII, Encyl. *Mystici Corporis:* "The communication of Christ's Spirit is the basis ... for the Church's becoming, so to speak, the plenitude and complement of the Redeemer: in the Church Christ in a sense reaches his fulfillment in all things (see Thomas Aquinas, *Comm. in epist. ad Eph*, 1, lect. 8). In this statement we have touched on the reason why ... the mystical Head who is Christ and the Church that on earth acts in his person as another Christ, form the one new being in which heaven and earth are joined to continue the saving work of the cross: when we say Christ, we mean the Head and the Body, the whole Christ": Denz-Schön 3813; AAS 35 (1943) 230-231.

See Augustine, *Enarrat. in Ps. 90*, 1: "Our Lord Jesus Christ is the total, complete man, both Head and Body: we acknowledge the Head in that man who was born of the Virgin Mary. . . . He is the Head of the Church. The Body of this Head is the Church, not the Church in this place but the Church here and the Church universal. Nor is it just the Church of today, but the Church from the time of Abel down to those to be born until the end of time who will believe in Christ, the entire holy people belonging to the one city. That city is Christ's Body and Christ is its Head": CCL 39, 1266; PL 37, 1159.

5. This means that Christ "who was without sin" "suffered for us";[14] "he was wounded for our offenses, crushed for our sins . . . by his stripes we were healed."[15]

Following in Christ's footsteps,[16] his faithful have always sought to assist each other along the road to the Father by prayer, spiritual kindnesses, and penitential expiation. The more ardent the charity motivating them, the more closely they have followed Christ in his suffering by bearing their own cross in atonement for their own sins and the sins of others and with the conviction that in the eyes of the Father of mercies they could be of service to the salvation of their brothers and sisters.[17] This, of course, is the ancient dogma of the communion of saints, namely, that the life of

---

[14] See 1 Pt 2:22 and 21.

[15] See Is 53:4-6 with 1 Pt 2:21-25. See also Jn 1:29; Rom 4:25 and 5:9ff.; 1 Cor 15:3; 2 Cor 5:21; Gal 1:4; Eph 1:7ff.; Heb 1:3, etc.; 1 Jn 3:5.

[16] See 1 Pt 2:21.

[17] See Col 1:24: "Now I rejoice in my sufferings for your sake and in my flesh I complete what is lacking in Christ; afflictions for the sake of his Body, that is the Church."

See Clement of Alexandria, *Lib. Quis dives salvetur* 42: St. John the Apostle urges a young thief to repentance, exclaiming: "I will be responsible to Christ for you. If necessary, I will gladly undergo your death, even as the Lord took on death for our sake. I will give my life as the substitute for yours": GCS, *Clemens* 3, 190; PG 9, 650.

See Cyprian, *De lapsis* 17, 36: "We believe that the merits of the martyrs and the words of the just have great power before the judge—but at the coming of judgment day, when, after the end of the present world, Christ's people will stand before his throne." "Whatever the martyrs have entreated and the priests have done for them can bring merciful forgiveness and be favorable on behalf of those who repent, work, and plead": CSEL 3, 249-250 and 263; PL 4:495 and 508.

See Jerome, *Contra Vigilantium* 6: "You say in your book that while we are alive we can pray for each other, but after we have died no one's prayer for another is to be heard: you say this especially because the martyrs could not do so even using the avengement of their own blood as an appeal (Rv 6:10). But if the apostles and martyrs when still in the body and in need of being concerned about themselves can pray for others, how much more so after their crown, their victory, and their triumph?": PL 23, 359.

See Basil the Great, *Homilia in Martyrem Julittam* 9: "We must weep therefore with those who weep. When you see others grieving out of repentance for their sins, shed tears with them, share in their grieving. The evils in others will enable you to correct what is wrong in yourselves. For those who shed scalding tears for the sins of their neighbors are healed themselves as they weep for others. . . . Grieve over sin: it is the sickness of the soul, the death of the deathless soul: sin calls for sorrow and unremitting laments": PG 31, 258-259.

See John Chrysostom, *In epist. ad Philipp.* 1, hom. 3, 3: "Therefore let us not as a matter of course grieve over those who die nor rejoice over the living. What then? Let us grieve over sinners not only as they die but while they live; let us rejoice over the just not only while they live but also after they have died": PG 62, 203.

each of God's children is in Christ and through Christ conjoined with the life of all other Christians.[18] That sublime bond exists in the supernatural unity of the Mystical Body of Christ and constitutes the one mystical person.[19]

That is the basis of the "treasury of the Church."[20] The treasury of the Church is not to be likened to a centuries-old accumulation of material wealth. It means rather the limitless and inexhaustible value that the expiations and merits offered by Christ have in the eyes of God for the liberation of all humanity from sin and for the creation of communion

---

See ST 1a2ae, 87.8: "If we speak of an expiatory punishment, one that we take on ourselves, then there are instances where one person bears the punishment due to another by reason of a bond between them. . . . If we are speaking of a punishment as it is inflicted for sin and as it has a fully penal quality, then a person is punished only for his own sin, because sinning is a personal act. If we speak of a punishment that is remedial, here too it may happen that a person is punished for another's sin. We have already determined that adversities in regard to possessions or even the body itself are in a way punitive remedies pointed toward salvation. Hence there is nothing against someone's being afflicted with such punishments either by God or by man for another's sin."

[18] See Leo XIII, Encyl. Epistle *Mirae caritatis:* "The communion of saints means precisely . . . the communication of mutual help, expiation, prayers, and kindnesses. This communication takes place between all the faithful, whether those in the bliss of heaven, those bound by the fires of purification, or those still on their earthly pilgrimage; all together they form the one city, whose Head is Christ and whose charter is charity": *Acta Leonis XIII* 22 (1902) 129; Denz-Schön 3363.

[19] See 1 Cor 12:12-13: "For as the body is one and has many members and all the members of that one body, being many, are one body, so also is Christ. For by one Spirit we are all baptized into one Body."

See Pius XII, Encycl. *Mystici Corporis:* "Thus [Christ] in some way lives in the Church so that the Church is like Christ's other self. Writing to the Corinthians, St. Paul asserts this when, without qualification, he calls the Church 'Christ' (see 1 Cor 12:12); he does so in imitation of his Master, who had cried out to Paul when he was the scourge of the Church: 'Saul, Saul, why do you persecute me?' (see Acts 9:4, 22:7, 26:14). To take it on the word of St. Gregory of Nyssa, St. Paul frequently calls the Church 'Christ' (see *De vita Moysis:* PG 44, 385); and you know well, revered brothers, the saying of Augustine 'Christ preaches Christ' (see *Sermones* 354, 1: PL 39, 1563)": AAS 35 (1943) 218.

See ST 3a, 48.2 ad 1 and 49, 1.

[20] See Clement VI, Jubilee Bull *Unigenitus Dei Filius:* "The only-begotten Son of God . . . gained a treasure for the Church militant. . . . Christ entrusted this treasury to be dispensed to the faithful . . . through St. Peter, the bearer of the keys of heaven, and his successors, Christ's vicars on earth. . . . The merits of the Blessed Mother of God and of all the elect from the first of the just to the last are recognized as supplementing the building up of this treasury . . .": Denz-Schön 1025, 1026, 1027.

See Sixtus IV, Encycl. Epistle *Romani Pontificis:* ". . . We who have received the fullness of power from on high, wishing to bring help and suffrage to the souls in purgatory from the universal Church's treasury, which consists of the merits of Christ and the saints and is entrusted to us . . .": Denz-Schön 1406.

See Leo X, Decr. *Cum postquam* to Cajetan de Vio, Papal Legate: ". . . to distribute the treasury of the merits of Jesus Christ and the saints . . .": Denz-Schön 1448; see Denz-Schön 1467 and 2641.

with the Father. The treasury of the Church is Christ the Redeemer himself: in him the atonement and merit of his redemption exist and are at work.[21] Added to this treasure is also the vast, incalculable, ever increasing value in God's eyes of the prayers and good works of the Blessed Virgin Mary and all the saints. As they followed Christ through the power of his grace, they became holy and they have accomplished a work pleasing to the Father. As a result, in working out their own salvation they have also contributed to the salvation of their brothers and sisters in the unity of the Mystical Body.

"All those who belong to Christ, possessing his Spirit, come together into the one Church and are joined together in Christ (see Eph 4:16). The union between those who are still pilgrims and the brothers and sisters who have died in the peace of Christ is therefore not broken, but rather strengthened by a communion in spiritual blessings; this has always been the faith of the Church. Because those in heaven are more closely united with Christ, they ground the whole Church more firmly in holiness . . . and in many ways contribute to its upbuilding (see 1 Cor 12:12-27). For after they have been received into their heavenly home and are present to the Lord (see 2 Cor 5:8), through him and with him and in him they do not cease to intercede with the Father for us, showing forth in the merits they have won on earth through the one Mediator between God and us (see 1 Tm 2:5), by serving God in all things and filling up in their flesh those things that are lacking of the sufferings of Christ for his Body which is the Church (see Col 1:24). Thus their familial concern brings great aid to our weakness."[22]

Thus between all the faithful—those in the bliss of heaven, those expiating for their sins in purgatory, and those still pilgrims on earth—there exists the continuing bond of charity and a rich interchange of all those good

---

[21] See Heb 7:23-25, 9:11-28.
[22] LG no. 49 [DOL 4 no. 157].

actions that, as atonement is made for the sins of the entire Mystical Body, appeases divine justice. At the same time divine mercy is moved to grant pardon in order that contrite sinners may more speedily reach complete possession of the blessings of God's family.

III

6. Aware of these truths right from its beginnings, the Church recognized and understood various ways of applying to its individual members the effects of the Lord's redemption, as well as ways for all its members to cooperate in the salvation of the others. This was how the whole Body of the Church was to be fitly joined together in righteousness and holiness for the full coming of God's kingdom, when he will be all things in all.

The apostles themselves urged their disciples to pray for the salvation of sinners.[23] The Church has unfailingly preserved this practice of its earliest days.[24] This has especially occurred in the pleas of penitents for the intercession of the entire community[25] and in suffrages on behalf of

---

[23] See Jas 5:16: "Confess your faults one to another and pray one for another, that you may be healed. The effectual, fervent prayer of a righteous man avails much."

See 1 Jn 5:16: "If anyone sees another commit a sin not deserving of death, he shall ask and God will give life for those whose sin is not unto death."

[24] See Clement of Rome, *Ad Cor.* 56.1: "Let us therefore also pray for those who are involved in any kind of sin, that restraint and humility may be given to them. Not that they should yield to us but to God's will. Thus the remembrance of them before God and the saints will be profitable to them and effective": Funk PA 1, 171.

See *Martyrium S. Polycarpi* 8, 1: "Finally he had finished his prayer, in which he had mentioned all those who at any time had come into contact with him, the small and the great, the famous and the unknown, and those belonging to the entire Catholic Church throughout the world . . .": Funk PA 1, 321, 323.

[25] See Sozomen, *Hist. Eccl.* 7,16, who says that in public penance after the celebration of Mass, penitents in the Church at Rome "cast themselves on the ground in groans and laments. Then the bishop, coming toward them in tears, also prostrates himself; and, confessing as one, the whole assembly of the Church weeps. Then the bishop rises first and bids the prostrate penitents rise. After prayers for the penitent sinners, as is proper, the bishop dismisses them": PG 67, 1462.

the dead, above all by the offering of the eucharistic sacrifice.[26] Also from earliest times in the Church the practice has existed of offering to God for the salvation of sinners good works, and in particular those that are more difficult for human frailty.[27] Because the sufferings of martyrs for the faith and for God's law were held in such high esteem, penitents used to ask their intervention so that, assisted by the merits of these confessors of the faith, they would more quickly be granted reconciliation by the bishops.[28] The high value set on the prayers and good works of the just led to the statement that the help of the whole Christian people cleaned, purified, and redeemed the penitent.[29]

---

[26] See Cyril of Jerusalem, *Catechesis* 23 (*mystag.* 5) 9, 10: "[We pray] then also for our deceased holy fathers and bishops and collectively for all who lived their lives among us. For we believe that this will be a great help to those souls for whom we pray while the holy and majestic victim lies in our presence." Confirming his point by the example of a crown being fashioned for an emperor to obtain his pardon for those driven into exile, Cyril concludes his sermon, saying: "Similarly in praying to God for the dead, even if they were sinners, we do not present him with a crown; rather we offer Christ who was sacrificed for our sins, pleading with the merciful God to relent and be gracious both to them and to us": PG 33, 1115 and 1118.

See Augustine, *Confessiones* 9, 12, 32: PL 32, 777; 9, 11, 27: PL 32, 775; *Sermones* 172, 2: PL 38, 936; *De cura pro mortuis gerenda* 1, 3: PL 40, 593.

[27] See Clement of Alexandria, *Lib. Quis dives salvetur* 42 [St. John the Apostle at the conversion of the young thief]. "Now pleading with God, now struggling along with the young man by prolonged fasts and with many sweet words softening his spirit, John did not give up, as they say, until he had brought him by persevering constancy into the Church . . .": GCS 17, 189-190; PG 9, 651.

[28] See Tertullian, *Ad martyres* 1, 6: "Some in the Church who lacked this pardon used to request it of the martyrs in prison": CCL 1, 3; PL 1, 695.

See Cyprian, *Epist.* 18 (or 12), 1: "We must, I think, do something about our brothers and sisters who have received certificates of pardon [*libelli pacis*] from the martyrs . . . that after the imposition of penance, they may come to the Lord with the pardon that they sought to receive through letters written to us by the martyrs": CSEL 3, 2, 523-524; PL 4, 265; see also *idem*, *Epist*, 19 (or 13), 2: CSEL 3, 2, 525; PL 4, 267.

See Eusebius of Caesarea, *Hist. Eccl.* 1, 6, 42: GCS, *Eus.* 2, 2, 610; PG 20, 614-615.

[29] See Ambrose, *De paenitentia* 1, 15: ". . . One who is rescued from sin by the prayers and tears of the people and purged inwardly is like one who is cleansed by the words of a whole people and washed by their tears. For Christ's gift to his Church is that one may be redeemed by all; the Church received the gift of Christ's own coming so that all would be redeemed by one": PL 16, 511.

In all of this, however, there was no thought that the individual members of the Church were acting through their personal powers for the pardon of the sins of others. The belief rather was that the Church itself precisely as it is the one Body joined to Christ as Head made expiation in its individual members.[30]

The Church of the Fathers held the absolute conviction that it carried out this salvific work in the communion of its pastors and under their authority; the Holy Spirit placed them as bishops to shepherd the Church of God.[31] Upon careful consideration of all the issues, the bishops established the manner and measure of expiation to be offered. They even gave permission for the satisfaction of canonical penances by means of other works perhaps less onerous, suited to the good of the whole community or contributing to devotion. Such works were to be performed by penitents themselves or even in some cases by others of the faithful.[32]

---

[30] See Tertullian, De paenitentia 10, 5-6: "The Body can find no joy in the trouble of one member, the whole must grieve together and seek for a remedy. The Church is in each one and the Church is Christ: therefore when you plead with your brothers and sisters, you plead with Christ and entreat him. So too when they shed tears over you, Christ is sorrowing, Christ is imploring the Father. What a son asks is always readily obtained": CCL 1, 337; PL 1, 1356.

See Augustine, Enarrat. in Ps. 85, 1: CCL 39, 1176-77; PL 37, 1082.

[31] See Acts 20:28. See also Council of Trent, sess. 23, Decr. de sacramento ordinis cap. 4: Denz-Schön 1768. Vatican Council I, sess. 4. Dogm. Const. De Ecclesia Pastor aeternus cap. 3: Denz-Schön 3061. LG no. 20: AAS 57 (1965) 23; ConstDecrDecl 126-128.

See Ignatius of Antioch, Ad Smyrnaeos 8, 1: "Let no one do anything related to the Church except joined to the bishops.": Funk PA 1, 283.

[32] See Council of Nicaea I, can. 12: ". . . those who by fear and tears and patience and good works give proof of their conversion in deed and in attitude, rightly will be received into the communion of prayers when the preestablished time of their probation is up, together with whatever work the bishop has the right to determine in kindness concerning them . . .": Mansi 2, 674.

See Council of Neo-Caesarea can. 3: Mansi 2, 540.

See Innocent I, Epist. 25, 7, 10: PL 29, 559.

See Leo the Great, Epist. 159, 6: PL 54, 1138.

See Basil the Great, Epist. 217 (canonica 3), 74: "A person who has fallen into the sins mentioned may by repenting become good again and the one who has been entrusted by God with the power of binding and loosing may, in view of the greatness of the sinner's repentance, show clemency in reducing the time of punishment. This clemency would not deserve condemnation because the accounts in Scripture teach us that those who do penance with greater ardor quickly receive God's mercy": PL 32, 803.

See Ambrose, De paenitentia 1, 15 (in note 29).

IV

7. Thus in the Church the abiding conviction has continued that the pastors of the Lord's flock could free the faithful from the remains of their sins by applying the merits of Christ and the saints. That conviction led gradually over the centuries through the inspiration of the Holy Spirit, who is the constant life-source of the people of God, to the practice of indulgences. The practice represents development, not departure, in the doctrine and discipline of the Church;[33] it is a new blessing, deriving from revelation as its root, introduced for the advantage of the faithful and of the whole Church.

The practice of indulgences spread gradually. It became a clear element in the history of the Church, above all when the popes decreed that certain works conducive to the good of the entire Church community "were to be regarded as having value for every kind of penance."[34] Further, the popes, "relying on the mercy of almighty God . . . and on the merits and authority of his apostles," granted "out of the fullness of apostolic power" not only full and generous, but absolute pardon for sins to the faithful who, "after true repentance and confession," performed such works.[35]

For "the only-begotten Son of God . . . gained a treasury for the Church militant. Christ entrusted this treasury to be

---

[33] See Vincent of Lerins, *Commonitorium primum* 23: PL 50, 667-668.

[34] See Council of Clermont, can. 2: "If anyone out of devotion alone and not to gain honor or money goes to Jerusalem to liberate the Church of God, that journey is to be regarded as a complete act of penance": Mansi 20, 816.

[35] See Boniface VIII, Bull *Antiquorum habet:* "The reliable records of the ancients show that great pardons and indulgences for sins were granted to those journeying to St. Peter's Basilica in Rome. Therefore . . . , regarding with favor all and each one of these pardons and indulgences as estabished, we confirm and approve them by apostolic authority. Relying on the mercy of almighty God and the merits of his apostles, on the counsel of our brothers, and on the fullness of our own apostolic power, we will and do grant this year and every future one-hundredth year not only full and generous pardon, but absolute pardon for sins to all . . . who devoutly journey to those basilicas, after repenting and confessing . . .": Denz-Schön 868.

dispensed for the well-being of the faithful through St. Peter, the bearer of the keys of heaven, and his successors, Christ's vicars on earth. This treasury is to be applied with mercy to those who are repentant and have confessed, on the basis of proper and reasonable causes, in some cases for total and in others for partial remission of the temporal punishment due to sin. The application may be either universal or for a particular case (according to what, in the Lord, the popes decide to be best). The merits of the blessed Mother of God and of all the saints . . . are recognized as supplementing these riches of the treasury of the Church."[36]

8. "Indulgence" is the name proper to this remission of the temporal punishment due to sins already forgiven as to their culpable element.[37]

An indulgence has certain features in common with other methods and means of taking away the remnants of sin, but at the same time is clearly distinct from the others.

This means that in the case of an indulgence the Church, using its power as minister of Christ the Lord's redemption, not only offers prayer, but authoritatively dispenses to the faithful rightly disposed the treasury of

---

[36] Clement VI, Jubilee Bull *Unigenitus Dei Filius:* Denz-Schön 1025, 1026, 1027.

[37] See Leo X, Decr. *Cum postquam:* ". . . we have decided to inform you that the Roman Church, which the other Churches are obliged to look to as a mother, has taught the following. The pope, successor of St. Peter the keybearer and the vicar of Jesus Christ on earth, possesses the power of the keys. Those keys are able to open the kingdom of heaven by taking away impediments to heaven existing in the faithful, namely, sin and the temporal punishment due to actual sin. The sin is taken away through the sacrament of penance; the temporal punishment, due according to divine justice for actual sins, through an ecclesiastical indulgence. Therefore to the faithful, who by the union of charity are Christ's members, whether they are in this life or in purgatory, the pope can, for reasonable cause, grant indulgences out of the superabundance of the merits of Christ and the saints. In granting an indulgence by his apostolic authority on behalf of both the living and the dead, the pope can distribute the treasury of the merits of Christ and the saints, confer an indulgence by way of absolution, or transfer it by way of suffrage, as is customary. Therefore all, both the living and the dead, who have truly gained all such indulgences are freed from the temporal punishment due according to God's justice for their actual sins in the measure equal to the indulgences they have gained": Denz-Schön 1447-48.

the expiatory works of Christ and the saints for the remission of temporal punishment.[38]

The purpose intended by ecclesiastical authority in granting indulgences is not only to help the faithful to pay the penalties due to sin, but also to cause them to perform works of devotion, repentance, and charity—especially works that contribute to the growth of faith and the good of the community.[39]

The faithful who apply indulgences as suffrages for the dead are practicing charity in a superior way and with their thoughts on the things of heaven are dealing more virtuously with the things of earth.

The Church's magisterium has defended and declared this teaching in various documents.[40] The practice of indulgences has sometimes been infected with abuses. This has happened because "rash and excessive indulgences" have led to contempt for the keys of the Church and to the

---

[38] See Paul VI, Letter *Sacrosancta Portiunculae:* "An indulgence granted by the Church to penitents is an expression of the wonderful communion of saints that mystically binds together by the one bond of Christ's charity the Blessed Virgin Mary and the assembly of Christ's faithful, whether triumphant in heaven, abiding in purgatory, or journeying on earth. An indulgence given through the Church either lessens or completely wipes out the punishment that in some way prevents us from attaining a closer union with God. Therefore the faithful who are repentant find in this special form of ecclesial charity the present help by which they may put off their old self and become a new being 'which is renewed in knowledge after the image of him that created it' (Col 3:10)": AAS 58 (1966) 633-634.

[39] See ibid.: "The Church reaches out to those faithful of Christ who, moved by repentance, seek to achieve after sin this *metanoia* by striving for that holiness which they first put on through their baptism in Christ. The Church by granting indulgences lends the support and assistance of a maternal embrace to its weak and frail children. An indulgence is not therefore an easy way out, whereby we may avoid the repentance required for sins. Rather it is a support that all the faithful, fully conscious in humility of their sins, find in the Mystical Body of Christ, which 'by charity, example, and prayer seeks their conversion' (LG no. 11)": AAS 58 (1966) 632.

[40] Clement VI, Jubiliee Bull *Unigenitus Dei Filius:* Denz-Schön 1026.

Clement VI, Letter *Super quibusdam:* Denz-Schön 1059.

Martin V, Bull *Inter cunctas:* Denz-Schön 1266.

Sixtus IV, Bull *Salvator noster:* Denz-Schön 1398.

Sixtus IV, Encycl. *Epistle Romani Pontificis provida:* "Wishing through our letters to correct . . . such scandals and errors . . . , we have written . . . prelates that they explain to the faithful the meaning of the plenary indulgence granted by us as a suffrage on behalf of the souls in purgatory. It does not mean that through this indulgence the faithful are discouraged from devout and good works; it means that the indulgence can be helpful as a suffrage for the salvation of souls. In that way the indulgence would profit these souls as though devout prayers were said and alms given in behalf of their salvation. We did not and do not intend, nor would we wish the

weakening of penitential expiation,[41] and because "fraudulent appeals for money" have brought curses upon the very name of indulgences.[42] The Church, however, uprooting and correcting abuses, "teaches and prescribes that the practice of indulgences, so beneficial to the Christian people and sanctioned by the authority of the sacred councils, must be preserved; the Church anathematizes those who state

---

inference to be made, that the indulgence does no more good or has no more effect than almsgiving and prayer or that almsgiving and prayer do as much good or have as great an effect as an indulgence by way of suffrage. We very well know that there is a great difference between prayer or almsgiving and such an indulgence. We stated that the indulgence has its effect *'perinde'* meaning 'in that way,' *'ac si,'* that is, in the way that prayer and almsgiving have an effect. And because prayer and almsgiving have their effect as suffrages offered for souls, in our desire to bring help and suffrage to the souls in purgatory, we, to whom the fullness of power has been given from above, have granted the indulgence in question out of the treasury of the universal Church, which consists in the merits of Christ and the saints and has been entrusted to us . . .": Denz-Schön 1405-06.

Leo X, Bull *Exsurge Domine:* Denz-Schön 1467-72.

Pius VI, Const. *Auctorem fidei* prop. 40: "The statement that 'an indulgence in its precise meaning amounts to the remission of a part of that penance that had been established canonically'—as though to say that an indulgence besides being simply the remission of a canonical punishment does not have the effect of pardoning the temporal punishment due according to divine justice for actual sins—is false, rash, contemptuous of the merits of Christ, and long ago included in the condemnation of Luther's art. 19": Denz-Schön 2640.

Ibid.: "Likewise the continuation of that proposition: 'the scholastics, puffed up by their subtleties, have proposed the misunderstood treasury of the merits of Christ and the saints and have replaced the clear notion of absolution from canonical penalty with the confused and false notion of the application of merits—as though to say that the treasury of the Church, the source of the pope's granting indulgences, does not consist in Christ's and the saints' merits'—is false, rash, contemptuous of the merits of Christ and the saints, and long ago included in the condemnation of Luther's art. 17": Denz-Schön 2641.

Ibid., prop. 42: "Likewise what follows: 'still more lamentable is the intention that this fanciful application be transferred to the dead'—is false, rash, offensive to the devout, contemptuous of the popes and the practice and mind of the Church universal, leading to the error qualified as heretical in Peter of Osma, and also already condemned in Luther's art. 22": Denz-Schön 2642.

Pius XI, Indiction of the Extraordinary Holy Year *Quod nuper:* ". . . mercifully in the Lord we grant and impart a full indulgence of all punishment due for sin to those who have first obtained remission and pardon of each of their own sins": AAS 25 (1933) 8.

Pius XII, Indiction of the Universal Jubilee *Iubilaeum maximum:* "We mercifully in the Lord grant and impart a full indulgence and pardon for all punishment due to sin to all the faithful during the course of this Holy Year, who, after they have duly atoned for their sins through the sacrament of penance and received communion, . . . devoutly visit . . . the Roman basilicas . . . and recite . . . prayers": AAS 41 (1949) 258-259.

[41] See Lateran Council IV, cap. 62: Denz-Schön 819.
[42] See Council of Trent, *Decr. de indulgentiis:* Denz-Schön 1835.

that indulgences are useless or who deny the Church's power to grant them."[43]

9. The Church today still invites all its children to weigh well and reflect on the real effectiveness of the practice of indulgences in fostering the life of individuals and of the Christian community as a whole.

To mention only the main points: this practice teaches us first "how evil and bitter it is to forsake . . . the Lord God."[44] For when the faithful gain indulgences they realize that by their own powers they cannot atone for the evil that they have inflicted upon themselves and the entire community by sinning; they therefore are moved to a healthy humility.

Next, the practice of indulgence teaches us the closeness of the union in Christ that binds us together and the extent to which the supernatural life of each person can contribute to others so that they too may be united more easily and more closely to the Father. Thus the practice of indulgences effectively enkindles charity in us and is an exceptional exercise of charity when it brings help to those asleep in Christ.

10. In addition, the usage of indulgence builds up confidence and hope for full reconciliation with God the Father. Yet this occurs in such a way that the practice provides no basis for negligence nor in any way lessens the concern to develop those dispositions required for full communion with God. Indulgences are indeed freely given favors, but they are granted both to the living and the dead only on fulfillment of certain conditions: to gain them the requirement on the one hand is the performance of good works, and on the other the faithful's having the necessary dispositions, namely, love for God, hatred toward sin, trust in the merits of Christ the Lord, and the firm belief that the communion of saints is of great advantage to the faithful.

---

[43] Ibid.
[44] Jer 2:19.

Nor must we omit that in gaining an indulgence the faithful submit themselves with docility to the lawful pastors in the Church, above all to the successor of St. Peter, the bearer of the keys of heaven. Christ himself has commanded these pastors to feed and shepherd his Church.

Thus it is that the salutary establishment of indulgences contributes in its own way toward presenting the Church to Christ without stain or wrinkle, but holy and undefiled,[45] and joined wondrously together in Christ by the supernatural bond of charity. Through indulgences the members of the Church, while being purified, advance more rapidly toward union with the heavenly Church. Therefore through indulgences the kingdom of Christ is being increasingly and more quickly established "till we all come into the unity of this faith and of the knowledge of the Son of God unto the point of our full perfection, according to the measure of the fullness of Christ himself."[46]

11. On the grounds of such truths, the Church once more recommends to its faithful the practice of indulgences as one dear to the Christian people throughout the many centuries and in our own times as well. At the same time the Church intends to take nothing away from other methods of sanctification and purification: above all the sacrifice of the Mass and the sacraments, and particularly the sacrament of penance, next the many helps that are included under the name of sacramentals, and finally devotional, penitential, and charitable works. All of these have in common that they sanctify and purify all the more effectively the closer a person is joined by charity to Christ the Head and to the Church his Body. The primacy of charity in the Christian life receives further confirmation by the teaching on indulgences. For they cannot be gained without genuine conversion (*metanoia*) and union with God, to which the performance of prescribed works is annexed. Thus the remission of

---

[45] See Eph 5:27.
[46] Eph 4:13.

penalties from the distribution of the Church's treasury is incorporated under the primacy of charity, which is maintained.

The Church appeals to the faithful not to abandon or make light of the traditions of the Fathers but to receive them reverently as a precious possession of the Catholic family and to honor those traditions. Nevertheless, the Church permits every person to use these resources of purgation and sanctification in the full freedom belonging to God's children. The Church ceaselessly reminds all the faithful of those things that must have priority in order to attain salvation because they are either the necessary things or the better and more effective.[47]

The Church at this time has seen fit to introduce new elements and decree new norms with regard to indulgences in order to enhance the value of this practice and the esteem for it.

V

12. The following norms introduce changes into the discipline of indulgences that are suited to the times and take into account the wishes of the conferences of bishops.

The regulations regarding indulgences in the *Codex Iuris Canonici* and the decrees of the Holy See remain unchanged to the extent that they are compatible with the new norms.

---

[47] See Thomas Aquinas, *In 4 Sent.* dist. 20, q. 1, a. 3, quaestiuncula 12.2 ad 2 (ST, Suppl., 25.2 ad 2): ". . . although such indulgences are of great worth for the remission of punishment, still, other works are more meritorious regarding the essence of our eternal reward: and this is infinitely better than the remission of temporal punishment."

The formulation of these norms has been concerned mainly with three points: to fix a new measure for partial indulgences; to lessen the number of plenary indulgences; to reduce and organize into a simpler and worthier form the matters related to indulgences attached to objects and places ("real and local" indulgences).

In regard to partial indulgences, in place of the ancient measure in days and years a new standard or measure has been set. According to it the act of the member of the Church who performs the indulgenced work is the criterion.

For by such an act the faithful can gain—in addition to merit, the chief effect of a good act—the remission of temporal punishment. That remission will be in proportion to the charity of the one acting and the value of the work done. Therefore it was decided to take this remission of punishment acquired by the faithful through their act as the measure of the remission of punishment that the supreme authority in the Church generously adds in the form of a partial indulgence.

As to plenary indulgences, it seemed advisable to reduce their number in a way that would be conducive to the faithful's right evaluation of them and helpful to their gaining them by being disposed in the required way. For the usual receives scant attention; the plentiful is not highly valued. Also many of the faithful need a time sufficient for a right preparation to gain a plenary indulgence.

As to "real" and "local" indulgences, two things were decided: a severe reduction in their number; the suppression of the very terms. The reason for the second is to make it clear that the Christian's acts are the subject of indulgences, not things or places; these are merely the occasions for gaining indulgences. Members of pious associations can gain the indulgences belonging to such associations by performing the prescribed works; the use of insignia is not a requirement.

NORMS

N. 1. An indulgence is the remission in the eyes of God of the temporal punishment due to sins whose culpable element has been taken away. The faithful who are rightly disposed and observe the definite, prescribed conditions gain this remission through the help of the Church, which, as the minister of redemption, authoritatively distributes and applies the treasury of the expiatory works of Christ and the saints.

N. 2. An indulgence is either plenary or partial accordingly as it frees a person either in whole or in part from the temporal punishment due to sins.

N. 3. Both partial and plenary indulgences are always applicable to the dead as suffrages.

N. 4. Henceforth a partial indulgence shall be designated by the words "partial indulgence" alone without any indication of days or years being added.

N. 5. Any of the faithful who, being at least inwardly contrite, perform a work carrying with it a partial indulgence, receive through the Church the remission of temporal punishment equivalent to what their own act already receives.

N. 6. A plenary indulgence may be gained only once on any day; the rule in N.18 regarding those on the verge of death is an exception.

A partial indulgence may be gained many times a day unless something different is explicitly stated.

N. 7. The requirements for gaining a plenary indulgence are the performance of the indulgenced work and the fulfillment of three conditions: sacramental confession; eucharistic communion; prayer for the pope's intentions. A further requirement is the exclusion of all attachment to sin, even venial sin.

Unless this unqualified disposition and the three conditions are present, the indulgence will be only partial; the prescription of N. 11 for those impeded is an exception.

N. 8. The three conditions may be carried out several days preceding or following performance of the prescribed work. But it is more fitting that communion and prayer for the pope's intentions take place on the day this work is performed.

N. 9. Several plenary indulgences may be gained on the basis of a single sacramental confession; only one may be gained, however, on the basis of a single communion and prayer for the pope's intentions.

N. 10. The condition requiring prayer for the pope's intentions is completely satisfied by reciting once the Our Father and Hail Mary for his intentions; nevertheless all of the faithful have the option of reciting any other prayer suited to their own devotion and their reverence for the pope.

N. 11. The faculty granted confessors by CIC can. 935 to commute for the benefit of those who are impeded either the prescribed work or the required conditions remains in force. But local Ordinaries may also grant to the faithful subject to them in keeping with canon law and who reside in places where they cannot go to confession or communion at all or can do so only with great hardship that they may gain a plenary indulgence without actual confession and communion, provided they have inner contrition and the resolution to receive these sacraments as soon as possible.

N. 12. The division of indulgences into "personal," "real," and "local" is no longer used. This is to make it clear that the subject of indulgences is the Christian's act, even though such an act sometimes has a connection with a particular object or place.

N. 13. The *Enchiridion indulgentiarum* is to be revised in such a way that indulgences will be attached only to major prayers and devotional, penitential, and charitable works.

N. 14. Lists and compilations of indulgences belonging to religious orders, congregations, societies of common life, secular institutes, and pious associations of the faithful shall be revised as soon as possible. This will result in the possibility of gaining a plenary indulgence only on special days fixed by the Holy See after a proposal in this regard has been made by the highest religious superior or by the local Ordinary in the case of pious associations.

N. 15. On 2 November a plenary indulgence, applicable exclusively to the dead, may be gained in all churches as well as in all public oratories and in all semipublic oratories — by those with a right to use them.

In all parish churches a plenary indulgence may be gained on two days in the year: the titular feast of the church and either on 2 August, the day of the "Portiuncula" indulgence or on another suitable day to be fixed by the Ordinary.

All the aforementioned indulgences may be gained either on the days already stipulated or, with the Ordinary's consent, on the Sunday preceding or following such days.

Other indulgences attached to churches or oratories shall be revised as soon as possible.

N. 16. The prescribed work for gaining an indulgence attached to a church or oratory is a devout visit there, which includes the recitation of the Lord's Prayer and the Creed (*Pater* and *Credo*).

N. 17. All the faithful gain a partial indulgence in devoutly using religious articles (crucifixes, crosses, rosaries, scapulars, medals) properly blessed by any priest.

All the faithful devoutly using a religious article blessed by the pope or by any bishop may also gain a plenary indulgence on the feast of the Apostles Peter and Paul; but they must add the profession of faith, recited in any approved formulary.

N. 18. It may happen that one of the faithful in danger of death is unable to have a priest to administer the sacraments and to impart the apostolic blessing with its attached plenary indulgence, mentioned in CIC can. 468, § 2. In such a case, the Church, like a devoted mother, graciously grants such persons who are properly disposed a plenary indulgence to be gained at the hour of death, provided they regularly prayed in some way during their lifetime. Use of a crucifix or cross is recommended for the gaining of this indulgence.

The faithful may gain this plenary indulgence at the hour of death even if they have already gained another plenary indulgence on the same day.

N. 19. The norms issued on plenary indulgences and especially those listed in N. 6, are applied also to those plenary indulgences that by custom hitherto have been called *toties quoties* indulgences.

N. 20. Like a devoted mother, the Church in its special concern for the faithful departed establishes that in every sacrifice of the Mass suffrages are most lavishly offered on behalf of the dead; any privilege in this matter is suppressed.

The effective date for the new norms regulating the gaining of indulgences is three months from the date on which this Apostolic Constitution appears in the *Acta Apostolicae Sedis.*

Indulgences attached to religious objects that are not mentioned in this Apostolic Constitution are suppressed three months after its publication in the *Acta Apostolicae Sedis.*

The revisions mentioned in N. 14 and N. 15 must be submitted to the Apostolic Penitentiary within one year. Two years from the date of this Apostolic Constitution indulgences that have not received confirmation will become null.

We will these our decrees and prescriptions to be and to remain established and in effect, notwithstanding, to the extent necessary, the constitutions and apostolic ordinances issued by our predecessors, and other prescriptions, even those worthy of special mention and amendment.

Hymni *Acathistos* recitatio

Recitation of the Akathist Hymn

In an audience granted to the Cardinal Major Peniten-tiary on 25 May 1991, the Holy Father Pope John Paul II, by his own supreme authority, approved the decree *Paeniten-tiariae Apostolicae* and ordered that it be published. The de-cree grants to the Christian faithful who recite the Akathist hymn the indulgence which for the utterly same reason is attached to the recitation of the Marian Rosary (cf. *Hand-book of Indulgences*, Grant no. 48).

INDEX